hey,

Welcome to this wonderful book brought to you by That Guy's House Publishing.

At That Guy's House we believe in real and raw wellness books that inspire the reader from a place of authenticity and honesty.

This book has been carefully crafted by both the author and publisher with the intention that it will bring you a glimmer of hope, a rush of inspiration and sensation of inner peace.

It is our hope that you thoroughly enjoy this book and pass it onto friends who may also be in need of a glimpse into their own magnificence.

Have a wonderful day.

Love,

Sean Patrick

That Guy.

Table of Contents

Introduction.. ix

Part I: How did I get here? 1

Chapter 1: You are an Addict 3

Chapter 2: What Happens in
Childhood Doesn't Stay in Childhood 13

Chapter 3: Rock Bottom...21

Chapter 4: What's at the Root?.............................33

Chapter 5: Discovering Your Toxic Seed 43

Chapter 6: A Deeper Commitment 63

Part II: Your Journey to Self-Love............................73

A New Day: Preparing for Your
30-Day Commitment 75

Day 1: Shifting the Focus to Me ∞..........................81

Day 2: The Power of Affirmations ∞......................93

Day 3: Be Here Now ∞ 107

Day 4: Mirror, Mirror on the Wall ∞....................115

Day 5: Perspective Shift ∞....................................123

Day 6: I Can See Clearly Now 131

Day 7: Say What You Mean,
Mean What You Say... 141

Day 8: The Power of Forgiveness.......................... 151

Day 9: The Conscious Inventory........................... 159

Day 10: You Can't Heal What You Don't Feel....... 175

Day 11: Tap it Out 183

Day 12: MYOB
(Mind Your Own Business), Really........................ 191

Day 13: Too Many Balls in the Air 199

Day 14: Pamper Yourself Because You Matter..... 211

Day 15: Jump, Laugh, Play.................................... 217

Day 16: Your Daily Practice ∞ 227

Day 17: Be Your Own Best Friend ∞ 235

Day 18: Celebrate Your Wins ∞ 243

Day 19: Respond Instead of Reacting ∞ 249

Day 20: Deactivate Your Triggers 257

Day 21: Protect Your Energy ∞............................. 265

Day 22: Speak Your Truth..................................... 273

Day 23: Trust Yourself,
The Answers are Within ∞ 281

Day 24: Detox from Distraction 289

Day 25: Get Connected 297

Day 26: Plug In ∞..305

Day 27: Your Looooooove Language 315

Day 28: Your Body is Your Temple ∞ 323

Day 29: A Whole New World ∞...........................333

Day 30: Get Naked ∞..341

Conclusion: Go Ahead, Dance
Naked in the Rain 349

Epilogue..351

Acknowledgments 353

About the Author 355

Introduction

If you're reading this book, you're the kind of person who generally solves everyone's problems for them. You're the 'go to' guy or gal. When crisis ensues, your brain immediately goes into solution mode. The moment the shit hits the fan you already have plan A in action and plan B and C are forming in your mind as back up. People look to you for advice and guidance and you like this feeling because you feel somewhat validated. You snap on the rescue cape without even realizing it because you want everyone around you to be content and taken care of. And, come on let's be honest, you prefer to handle things yourself because then at least you know it was done right.

This is all fine and dandy if this behavior is necessary for success in your career or if you are navigating small children through life, but when it comes to relationships – this is a one way, do not pass go, direct flight to HELL!

Ever wonder why you keep landing in these relationships where you feel the need to rescue other people?

You fall in love with the *idea* of them at first and then the red flags begin to pop up consistently. This is when something deep inside of you clicks and you say, '*I can fix them. I can and I will*!' You put your cape on and take on the rescuer role because you have determined that they are the victim and you can and will be their hero.

Whether it's a romantic relationship, a close friend, or a family member, you put all your time and energy into this person. You find yourself thinking or worrying about them constantly. You change your own plans to accommodate their needs even when they don't ask. You try hard to make things easier for them so they won't feel stressed or depressed. Unfortunately, before you know it, you're mentally, physically, and emotionally flipping drained. It's only then that you realize that something's not right and you have somehow become the victim and there's no-one to rescue you!

Sound familiar?

Well, welcome to my world, until one day I finally woke up and realized that I could no longer just hang the rescue cape in the closet for safe keeping until someone needed me. Instead, I needed to learn to rescue *myself*, burn that damn cape, and then go out and dance naked in the freakin' rain. That's right, I said dance naked in the rain. You know, dance like nobody's watching or like you really don't give a shit if they are! I'm talking about getting emotionally naked, being able to stand in front of a mirror, and love yourself for the bad, the good, and the indifferent. A deep understanding that you are perfect just as you are.

You see, when I finally hit my rock bottom I had no choice but to look in the mirror while I was completely naked and be very real with myself. There was no one standing in that mirror with me who was going to make it all better. The only person who could and would rescue me was the person staring back at me. That was crystal clear.

I knew then and there that everything was going to be okay because suddenly I was comfortable in my own skin. I finally knew in every fiber of my being that I would no longer allow toxic, deep-seated beliefs to prompt me to search outside of myself for approval. Nor would I seek or count on others to rescue me in my worst despair. The darkest point in my life was the only place I was finally able to see the light and a clear vision of who would always have my back.

Maybe that time has come for you. Perhaps you're tired of the emotional pain and feelings of unworthiness. Maybe the job of rescuing others has become tiresome for you and you're ready to learn to take care of the one person who will always appreciate your efforts.

If so, get ready to take a long, hard look in the mirror and once and for all ask what *your* needs are instead of striving to please others by rescuing them.

You think you might be ready to dance naked in the rain or at least willing to look in the mirror?

Then stand tall and let's get to it!

PART I:

How did I get here?

Chapter 1:
You are an Addict

So, you want to be a hero eh?

It feels good to know that you've helped someone, right? I mean, there's a definite rush in sensing that you have made a difference in someone else's life. It certainly feels good when someone notices you or appreciates the effort you put forth. It is amazing to be needed, wanted, or desired – especially when you feel that you've helped someone grow to another level.

The feelings that we experience from helping others are often euphoric and positive until we start chasing that high and looking for validation outside of ourselves by snapping on the rescue cape. Then, before you know it, your life is out of control and you suddenly don't even know who you are anymore. One day you're riding high on a wave, feeling pretty damn good because you're making a positive difference for someone else; you feel noticed, loved and appreciated.

The next day, you feel down in the dumps because they no longer seem to want your thoughts, ideas, or opinions. You now feel; invisible, unwanted and unappreciated. That is the roller coaster of emotions that we often experience when we snap on the cape and try so very hard to rescue others instead of taking care of ourselves.

I believe I had my cape fastened on tightly from the time I was a small child. I brought home all the strays (and I mean *all* the strays) and wanted to fix all the broken wings. I had a strong desire to be sure that everyone else was happy. My role in my family was the peace maker. I am absolutely – without a doubt – a rescuer.

Perhaps you are as well...

As a rescuer you see someone who you believe needs help and you want to be there for them, love them, attend to them and heal them. You see the good even in the evilest of people. I, myself, have always been really good at that. I can see the light in every single person I meet including – and not limited to – the most broken of them all. It always seems like a good idea at the time to rescue someone until you realize that 'seeing' the light and getting 'burned' by that light are dangerously close.

If you truly want to burn the damn cape and rescue yourself, then it's critical to understand why it's so important to be the hero and be clear about where your cape came from.

The Addiction

I'm going to start off strong. No sugar coating here. Let's get one thing straight, you, the rescuer, are an addict.

*What? Did she just tell me I'm an addict? That can't be true! I'm the one who dates the addict, is married to the addict, or perhaps takes care of the addict. I'm certainly **not** the addict.*

When you hear that word, 'addict', it most definitely catches you off guard. It seems dirty, sinister and shameful, but humor me for a moment here and let's see if the shoe fits.

Go ahead and google the definition for the word addict. The first definition that comes up is; *an addict is simply a person who is addicted to a particular substance.* Now, go ahead and dig deeper my friends and you'll see that *an addict is an enthusiastic devotee of a specified thing or activity.*

Hmmmmmmm. Something to think about. That seems to change the perspective a bit, doesn't it? I bet you can think of one person who you have enthusiastically been devoted to, correct?

You dedicate your time, energy, and sometimes money to this person who you believe you love so very much and want to help in any way you can. You are constantly thinking of this person, putting them first and putting your own needs on the back burner. They are the 'object of your affection', or perhaps your addiction?

Let's look at the definition of addiction now. Go ahead and Google that bad boy!

What you will find here is, *addiction is the fact or condition of being addicted to a particular substance, thing, or activity.*

Are you following me here?

Are you seeing that even though you may not necessarily be addicted to a substance per se, you are in fact addicted to an activity, thing, or person?

Okay, so now let's break it down and see what you are more specifically addicted to...

Are you addicted to 'fixing' others?

Do you find yourself constantly looking at ways to improve your spouse, close friends, family, or significant other? Do you dedicate your time and energy to the betterment of those around you instead of taking care of yourself? If so, you might just be addicted to the fix!

Are you addicted to validation?

Do you find yourself constantly scanning social media to see who liked your posts and what people are saying about you? Are you searching for approval from others to feel like you are accomplished, liked, or worthy in some way? If so, you may be addicted to the chase of being validated outside of yourself.

Are you addicted to drama?

Does your mind constantly wonder when the other shoe is going to drop? Do you find yourself playing out negative situations long before they even happen? Are you quick to tell 'your story' to everyone you meet or anyone who will listen? If so, you might just be addicted to life's drama.

Your addiction may be connected to one or all of the above. One thing I know for sure is that if you in fact can relate to the introduction of this book and consider yourself a rescuer, then you are certainly addicted to putting others first.

I know, I know, this all sounds a bit crazy to think of yourself as having an addiction to this cycle. All this time you've looked at yourself as the victim in these relationships. You've thought of yourself as being taken advantage of and felt violated and betrayed when you've done so much for the other person.

Well, hit the pause button for a moment and shift the focus. Then look in the mirror and ask yourself, is that really true? Am I truly a victim? Have I absolutely been taken advantage of, or have I willingly given my power over to someone or something (probably without even realizing it)?

Now, do you see why you are in fact an addict?

The Truth

Let's not look at addiction as a dirty word anymore. Instead, let's call it what it is. It's a sickness. It's the absence of joy because it comes from a place of lack. Addiction generally takes hold in our lives because we are missing something deep within our hearts.

When someone has an addiction, it absolutely consumes them. They begin to think about the object of their affection 24/7; nothing else compares for them. Somehow, they are convinced that if they have this substance, this activity or this thing, then everything else will suddenly feel right. Sadly, this is only a façade because when you are in the midst of addiction you are searching to fill a void and you always discover that the void is never satisfied. In fact, the more you focus on the addiction and fill yourself with this substance, activity, or thing, the emptier you feel.

As a rescuer, the person you believe you are rescuing is *your* object of affection. You tell yourself that you deeply care about and love this person and you don't want to see them fail or self-destruct. You convince yourself that everything you're saying and doing is for them. However, the truth is, you too are filling a void. And everything you're saying and doing is to get some type of validation from 'fixing' or saving someone else.

Guess what? It's really none of your business if they want to self-destruct.

If you truly love this person or care deeply for them, you will express what you see and feel in a healthy manner by sharing your concerns and directing them to a professional for help. You won't make excuses for them, try to please them, or lower your integrity for them. If you do any of that, you're simply enabling them and tethering yourself to a sinking ship.

Here's what I've learned. Let go of the anchor. If an anchor is sailing through the sky and heading for the deep blue sea, let that shit go! Unless of course you'd like to drown in the ocean of life because that's exactly what you're doing by holding on to toxic relationships and not taking care of your own needs.

For some of us we realize we are rescuers by the romantic relationships we land in. Maybe it's not a romantic relationship you're thinking of. Perhaps it's a relationship with a family member, coworker or friend. Maybe, just maybe, this is who you have become in *all* of your relationships. To be honest, if you can relate to being a rescuer in any of your relationships, then chances are this is a common thread throughout your life and it affects several connections for you.

Look, you came into this world alone; whether you're a twin, quintuplet, or singlet. You will also exit this world alone; whether you die in a room by yourself or in a catastrophic event with hundreds of thousands of people. Your journey from here to there is your own.

You can have an open heart, be loving and supportive of others to the best of your ability, but you cross the line when taking care of others takes away from your own well-being. That's when you know your cape is fastened tightly and it's time to rip it off, get the matches and watch that baby burn!

In reality, the number one relationship that's being deeply affected by snapping on the cape, is your relationship with yourself. You are worth more than you believe, and you deserve the very best. Your worth isn't dependent on what you can do to help others. However, you won't understand that until you take a long hard look in the mirror.

The irony of being a rescuer is that the rescuer believes that they truly want to rescue others. However, if you think about it critically, you really want to be rescued yourself.

Your deep need to rescue isn't for naught. This need is your own need to rescue the little kid deep within you. If you feel the need to rescue others, there is a critical need that was not met during your childhood. Your childhood is your foundation to your life and it holds the answers to healing the wounds within. The good news is, you can be rescued and you can be that hero you've always wanted to be. However, it's not for other people. Instead, you need to rescue yourself.

You have one final rescue to make before you burn the damn cape-rescuing that little kid within. If you're open to getting those matches ready, then we must take a trip down memory lane.

In the next few chapters, I'm going to get 'naked' to help you to feel comfortable when we all dance naked in the rain. Allow me to guide you gently by sharing my stories first, and then you'll look in the mirror for yourself.

Breathe deeply. You can do this. The first step to healing is awareness. Take off the rose-colored glasses and wipe the sandman out of your eyes. It's time to truly open your eyes and see what led you here and then choose a new path for your journey forward. And, oh by the way, you absolutely and totally deserve happiness. Let's go get it!

Chapter 2:

What Happens in Childhood
Doesn't Stay in Childhood

In my first book, "Ignite the Light: Empowering Children & Adults to Be Their Absolute Best," I discussed the importance of childhood at length. Childhood is our foundation. It is the ground level, the beginning of our journey and the root system to our tree of life! We are forming deep connections and an understanding of the world around us from the moment we are developing in utero until about age seven. This is where our belief system is born, and our subconscious brain creates messages that will play throughout our lifetime. If we don't have a strong foundation it certainly makes navigating the waters of life more difficult as adults.

A strong foundation is formed when we are taught to love ourselves, feel our feelings, quiet our minds, tune in to the voice within, remove toxic thoughts, speak our truth, and plug in to our higher self. Many of us are given some of these tools in childhood but of course not all.

I like to think of life as a garden. We are generally given the sun, water, and nutrients for our soil so we may grow a beautiful garden. Yet, inevitably a few 'weeds' sneak in there and if you don't stay on top of them and pull them from the root as you become aware of them, then they will overtake your garden of life. These weeds come from the voice of fear. This voice creates messages that you hear throughout your life somewhere deep inside of you and it often holds you back from attaining everything and anything you truly want, need, and desire. Under the voice is a core toxic belief. I work with clients to reveal this core toxic seed within our first session and this is all part of the three-step healing process that you will learn, but we'll dive into that a little further down the road.

The Approval Game

From the time we are infants we are taught to seek approval outside of ourselves. Think about this for a moment; when infants lift their heads for the first time, what do we do? We smile, we get excited and we applaud – especially if that infant is our own! When that infant crawls for the first time, what is it that we do? We smile, get excited and applaud. When that child walks, talks or reaches some accolade we generally show them that they've won our approval.

The child gets positive feedback and wants more so they continue to do what they think makes you happy because it feels good to them.

Now don't get crazy. I'm not saying that we shouldn't praise our children and show excitement when they achieve something. Instead, I'm simply stating where the general need for approval outside of ourselves originates. What I teach children (and the adults who raise them) is to first seek approval from within.

When a child comes to me to ask if I like their picture, their creation or something that they've done, I get down on their level (which isn't difficult because I'm 5'1"), look in to their eyes and simply say, "What do *you* think?"

The first few times they experience this with me they tilt their head like a brand-new puppy and look a bit confused. I guide them by asking more questions like, "What do you think about your picture? Do you like it?" They then begin to see that it's safe for them to express self-approval and the shift begins. As time goes on they no longer run to me to ask my opinion. Instead, they come to me and say something like, "Ms. Savini, look how good this tree is!" Or, "Did you see how amazing I did on the monkey bars?"

Most of us look for validation from others instead of deep within because we were not taught in our childhood to believe in ourselves, love ourselves unconditionally and speak our truth. Instead, we were taught to do what we were told, stuff our feelings, and avoid talking about what ails us.

As a rescuer, somewhere in our childhood we were taught that the only way to get validation was through the approval of others. We were taught that our needs, wants, and desires were not important but if we could meet the needs, wants, and desires of others, then we were visible, important and valued.

Bzzzzzzzzzzzz! Wrong answer! The truth of the matter is that by never focusing on our own needs, wants, and desires we have made ourselves vulnerable to pain, sadness, and despair.

The Toxic Seeds Take Root

We all have these toxic seeds that dwell deep within our hearts. Seeds that were unintentionally planted during early childhood. The sooner you discover *your* toxic seeds, the sooner you are able to initiate the healing process.

Let's look at that as I open my personal book of life to you...

I was not physically nor sexually abused as a child. I had two hard working, loving, amazing parents who did the very best they could, and I *still* have toxic seeds in my garden of life. For me, my biggest hurdle in life has been learning to put myself first.

As a young child I had my cape fastened on tightly. My role in my family was always clown and/or peace maker. I don't remember having an induction ceremony, but it was clear to me that my role was to make others happy by pleasing them in some way. This was the only time that I felt valued and visible.

I grew up in a home where my parents were do-gooders or people pleasers and my mom was the best damn martyr there ever was! My parents were always putting the needs of others before their own and therefore continually seeking approval outside of themselves.

My mom was in her mid 30's when she gave birth to me, and I was an 'accident' (they made no bones about that). I have three older sisters; 11, 15, and 16 years older than I am and so you can likely see how I was quite a surprise! My mom got married at 17 and became a mother at the ripe ol' age of 18. She never truly gave herself the time and attention she needed to heal her own wounds from childhood. By the time she gave birth to me, she was mentally, physically, and emotionally drained and feeling like a human *doing* instead of a human *being.* Life experience has shown me that she felt this way because she wasn't in touch with who she was outside of being a wife and mother.

My mom grew up in a somewhat 'unconventional' family in the 50's (although it's happenstance today). Her mother was married a few times, she had step siblings, and her father was an alcoholic. From a very young age she formed a toxic belief that she wasn't important and that she had to do certain things to be noticed, such as; be a good girl, don't disturb daddy, don't get in mommy's way. She married my dad at 17 to get away from her toxic home and perhaps find the emotional support she needed but didn't have at home.

My dad also came from an 'unconventional' family in that time period. He too had parents who had divorced and remarried, along with step siblings. On top of this, he suffered the loss of two siblings from two separate tragic events that shook the family to the core. My dad learned early that life was tough, and you had to be strong and take care of business. He had a twin who was ill and favored as a child and he learned to take care of others and put his own needs on the back burner. My dad always took the back seat to his twin brother and looked out for his younger sisters. He was their rock, but was never truly valued for his sacrifices. He learned early on that he was never going to be enough, therefore forming the toxic belief, I'm not enough.

As you can see, both of my parents were caretakers, a.k.a. rescuers. They came from different backgrounds with similarities, but ultimately, they each learned to take care of others to feel important and valued.

I think by this point you might be able to see how I joined the rescuer clan without having an awful childhood.

It absolutely raises the hair on the back of my neck when someone judges another and says, "What do you have to complain about, you had a perfect childhood?" In my case, this could be true. I had wonderful, amazing, hard-working, loving parents who did the very best they could. However, that doesn't mean that they gave me the foundation that I needed to be my absolute best self. How could they? They were carrying their own baggage through life's airport. Sooner or later the children were bound to jump in and carry that baggage as well!

My parents, your parents, all parents do the best they can with what they have to work with. I don't believe that any parent sets out to screw up their kid on purpose, but I also don't believe that you have to have a horrifically abusive childhood to be somewhat mixed up emotionally.

A toxic belief can come from a home like mine or a home where there is constant chaos and abuse. No matter what kind of home it comes from and what path was taken to get there, that deep toxic belief still *feels* the same. Whether you feel unworthy, unimportant, not enough, unlovable, or unsafe, the *feeling* is the same.

You may have grown up in a home where there was a great deal of arguing and you had to step in the middle of arguments to prevent disaster. This would certainly make you feel unsafe. On the other hand, you may have grown up in a home where your parents were loving and hard-working, but you had a lot of alone time because they were working to keep up with the Jones'. Either way, the feeling of being unsafe is the same feeling. Those feelings that develop from a young and tender age stick with us for the rest of our lives. If we believe that we are not enough, we will always strive to find approval outside of ourselves. If we believe that we are never safe, then we will most certainly be over cautious and afraid to take risks in life that could help us to grow beyond our barriers. If we believe that we are not lovable, then we will seek relationships that leave us feeling empty and unloved. No matter what the feeling is that we develop from these toxic beliefs in childhood, we will most definitely carry that into our future and use it like a map for our journey without even realizing we are doing so.

The bottom line is that when we exit childhood with these deep toxic beliefs we carry them into our adult life and they cause havoc. Allow me to show you how *my* toxic beliefs caused havoc in my life and ultimately revealed that it was time to burn the damn cape for my own sanity and self-preservation.

Chapter 3:
Rock Bottom

They say when you have an addiction, it's not until you truly hit rock bottom that you begin to heal. For me, that was accurate. I had to hit rock bottom – the darkest, coldest, loneliest place I had ever been – in order for my healing to begin.

I was married to a compulsive gambler for almost 12 years (together in the relationship for 16). There were other addictions as well for him but the true thorn in his side – and mine – was the compulsion to pick 'the winning team'. Sadly, he sucked at it, and his choice of his addiction over his family destroyed any chance we had of ever being a happy, healthy family.

We dated for four years prior to marriage and I definitely saw red flags early on but that rescuer voice in my head said, "It's okay. All good. You can fix him. You've got this. He's a good person deep inside and maybe you will be the difference for him" (that actually sickens me to write that today).

I spent the first few years of our relationship trying to understand why he would tell me one thing and do another, including telling me we were getting together and then completely blowing me off! I wondered why I put up with this but couldn't quite get to the toxic seed that was tethering me at this point. It was often clear that he was lying to me, yet I somehow made excuses for him because I was seeing him for *who I wanted him to be and not for who he truly was*. This was a delusional pattern I had to break to begin healing. I couldn't break that pattern until I came to the realization that I was betraying myself by putting others first.

For years I had no clue that gambling was the culprit. I kept looking at myself and asking what it was that I was doing wrong. I had this thought in my head that I wasn't enough to keep him interested, so he went out with his friends to "party". At this point in my life I had no idea about these pesky little toxic beliefs that were dwelling deep inside my heart and causing havoc (if I only knew then what I know now).

As rescuers we often make excuses for the behavior of others and put ourselves on the back burner.

While we dated over the course of four years, instead of looking in the mirror, realizing and taking care of my own worth, I kept the focus on him and tried to figure out why he lied to me. Then, I thought I figured it out, but was still convinced that my cape was golden and I could 'fix' him.

Got It All Figured Out

My ex-husband would gamble when he felt shitty about himself. In high school and college he was recognized and valued for his outstanding athletic ability. He never went as far as he would've liked to in sports, so he still needed some connection to sports to feel worthy. By placing bets on games, I believe he felt some sort of connection to the sports world and this brought him back to his glory days. In his mind he thought if he was still involved in some way then he'd still be recognized and valued. Unfortunately, he'd place those bets and then lose, and when he lost, he lost big. This only made him feel worse about himself. He was embarrassed and ashamed and so then he would use other substances as well to numb himself. It was an awful cycle to watch and I just wanted to love him, heal him, and help him. (Can you see my cape blowing in the breeze now?)

I was a small town, naïve, innocent young woman so I really didn't know much about this kind of life style. Perhaps that's why it took me so long to figure it all out. For all the accomplishments that I've made in my life I truly only wanted one thing; I wanted to be a wife and mother, and a damn good one at that. I just wanted a happy, healthy family.

Sadly, once I saw clearly and I understood that I was not going to be fixing him – because that was his choice and job to do – I knew I had to break free and take care of my son and I. As difficult as it was to give up my dream of a happy, healthy family, I did just that. I told him I wanted a divorce, we went to a mediator, sold the house, and I bought another home for my son and I to begin a new journey.

It was difficult to move forward with a divorce because I had to let go of the dream and had to come to an understanding that I couldn't help my ex-husband. That was the hardest part for me because by this point I was running a successful coaching business where people were breaking free from toxic beliefs formed in childhood and becoming the very best version of themselves.

I struggled for months trying to understand how I could help perfect strangers, but the man who slept in the bed next to me and who raised my son with me could not and would not accept my help. It was clear to me that my ex-husband's core toxic belief was that he was not enough, but I knew there was absolutely nothing I could do to help him see that or heal. It was time to move on and look at myself instead.

While striving to heal, I came to an understanding that perhaps *my* deepest toxic belief was that *I* was not enough or perhaps unworthy in some way of love. I focused my energy on myself for once and was able to let go of feeling like a failure because I couldn't help him and save our marriage or family. Perhaps that was the first step to burning the cape for me.

You would think that this experience would've been my rock bottom. I mean, all I ever wanted was to be married and have a happy, healthy family and this addiction made that impossible. However, that wasn't my rock bottom. There was more to come as the Universe wasn't quite finished teaching me how to truly love myself. I left that relationship with the sense that my core belief was, "I'm not enough," yet the next chapter of my life revealed that my core belief had deeper roots.

The Bottom of the Pit

Shortly after separating from my husband I met a man who I believed was my soul mate. We connected on every level (or so it seemed). He said everything I wanted to hear to revive that dream of a happy, healthy family once again. At first, upon meeting him, I was a bit hesitant because he seemed to want to move at lightning speed, but my vulnerability allowed for my heart to soften quickly with little effort on his part.

Let's give him the name of Richard and call him *Dick* for shits 'n giggles. Dick was a very charismatic man with eyes as blue as the sea and a coy smile that could draw in Medusa! He was incredibly intelligent and very well spoken. In the beginning he was somewhat shy around me and very complimentary. I think he drew me in by playing on my heart strings. He had an awful childhood and could easily read me. I'm quite sure he noticed that every time he spoke of his childhood, all I wanted to do was surround him in my loving arms and heal all his wounds. Maybe that was the draw in the beginning – once again, I believed I could be the hero.

It was about two weeks in when I saw the first red flag. I walked into his kitchen to throw something in the garbage and saw several empty liquor bottles in the trash. I didn't want to stare so I quickly closed the garbage and tried to put it out of my mind. He had owned several bars in the past and this flag made me wonder if there was a drinking problem. I danced around the topic for a bit and then asked him about the drinking and of course he had a great excuse as most addicts do. I asked him why he liked to go to bars so much and he said that he only went to bars to socialize with others because the job that he held was extremely isolating. He then assured me that when he was in a relationship he didn't go to bars unless he was with his partner. I quickly learned in the months that followed that this was a complete lie, as well as him not having a drinking problem.

Not long after this conversation I began to see a trail of lies. Things just didn't add up; he would tell me he was tired and going to sleep at 8:30 at night, he would text me and then I'd try to Facetime him a few seconds later and he wouldn't answer, and the list goes on. At about three weeks in I tried to talk to him about how his actions were making me feel. He put it back on me and said this was because of what I went through with my husband and I was projecting that onto him. We were Facetiming, I was crying my eyes out and he looked right at me and said, "I don't care about your feelings! You're making me feel like you don't trust me, and I can't be with someone who doesn't trust me!" Of course, as a rescuer, I backed down because I knew I wasn't pleasing him and I wanted more than anything to please him, heal him, and love him (I think I just vomited in my mouth on that one).

That should've been the end of the relationship and if my cape were in fact toast at that point it would've been the end, but oh no it wasn't. Instead I spent a little over a year and a half with this man learning more and more about him, suspecting not only alcohol addiction but also drug addiction, womanizing, and concluding that he was absolutely – beyond any shadow of a doubt – a narcissist. Yep, remember in the beginning of this book when I said I could see the best in even the most broken people? Well, there you have it.

That relationship had a terrible repetitive pattern; I would break up with him and then feel awful or he'd push me away and then draw me back in. I felt like I was tied to him in some way and I couldn't explain it. He was my drug, and perhaps I was his as well.

I remember he would say the most awful things to me and always put it back on me when I would question his intentions or whereabouts. I discovered that I continued to put up with this crap because I believed that I needed to know the truth to move on. This was sadly because I had learned to trust what others were saying and doing over what my own gut was telling me was true. Once again, I was betraying myself by seeing another man for who I wanted him to be instead of who he actually was.

I had finally gotten to a point where I decided that enough was enough and I didn't need to know the whole truth to release him, and that's when more truth ironically came out.

I was contacted by another woman and she revealed that the entire time we had been in (what I thought was a monogamous relationship) she had also been on and off with him, and oh by the way, there were other women as well!

After confronting him we both began the healing process to move on with our lives. She moved on quicker than I because I still wanted to believe that it wasn't true. I went back and forth with him for months even after this experience of finding out about other women. That's when you know you must heal your wounds – when you allow someone to walk all over you and you're still begging for their attention and love. After several months of anguish and despair, I finally took a long hard look in the mirror.

At first, I wondered how this could happen. How could I be so stupid and allow someone to take advantage of me not only in the same way my ex-husband had, but even worse? I beat up on myself and was disgusted not only with him, but mostly myself. As time went on and I began to truly heal with the work that I will share with you in this book, I was no longer disgusted with him. Instead, I was now thankful. I was thankful for seeing the truth. I was thankful for this God-awful experience, and I was thankful to have truly discovered my core toxic belief (roots and all) so I could finally heal. What is it they say? *"You can't heal what you don't feel!"*

It was through this relationship that I honestly hit *my* rock bottom to heal from this addiction of rescuing others. Gut wrenching, unbelievable pain in my heart made me finally look at myself and see why I was attracting this kind of man into my life. My core belief wasn't only that I somehow felt unworthy. The deeper belief was that I wasn't important and I had to dig deep to figure out why.

I had a very difficult summer that year. I experienced anxiety and depression at a level that I would never want to experience again. I could honestly say after going through all that emotional pain I finally understood why people turned to alcohol and drugs as a means to alleviate their pain. I truly wanted to just ease the pain and run away, but I didn't. Instead,

I felt my feelings day after miserable day. I went through ups and downs, wanting him in my life, and then realizing how toxic he was for me. Push and pull, push and pull. I reached out to friends to seek comfort and understanding, but even the best of friends could not console me because they could not understand my pain and didn't have the tools to heal me. It wasn't just the end of this relationship that drove me to the bottom of that pit. Instead, it was a deep understanding that I was putting myself on the back burner to please someone else. Connected to that was a sense that no one in the world could truly get me through this or help me; not a therapist, not my mom, not my sisters, not my friends, not even my adorable little dogs. There was no one who could get me through this pain because the only remedy that would truly heal this cancer within me was standing completely naked, rolling my shoulders back, putting my eyes forward, looking in the mirror, and once and for all loving myself for the good, the bad, and the indifferent.

Falling into the pit of hell and sucking down tons of dirt was one of the most difficult challenges of my life, but it forced me to come to an understanding that the one person who would always have my back was me. It was now time to take really good care of the woman staring back at me in the mirror not only to avoid toxic relationships, but to give myself the love and support I truly deserved. That's when I began to work the program I'm going to share with you in this book and amazingly, that's when everything in my life changed for the better.

Reflection

When you think back to what I shared about my childhood you can likely see where this came from. I was always pleasing and taking care of others; my value was determined by pleasing others and making them happy. That is what I was taught to do. I never took the time to define my needs, wants, or desires. Instead, I just accepted what was given to me and asked how I could serve.

Being a loving, kind person who wants to love those who have pain is not terrible in and of itself. What is detrimental though is not defining your own needs, wants, and desires, and putting yourself last.

You see, if I had known that my core belief was that I wasn't important, I could've worked to heal that, and *Dick* would've never been attractive to me. I may have cared for him or even felt sorry for him, but I certainly would have never formed a relationship with him that lasted almost 2 years! I wouldn't have done that because I would've seen my importance in this life and it would've been very clear to me that 'he didn't give a shit about my feelings'.

Listen, when someone tells you who they are, believe them! He told me he didn't care about my feelings at week three and I sadly disregarded that and made excuses for him.

I had to hit a rough rock bottom to heal but perhaps you don't. If I only had taken the time to truly look in the mirror a long time ago to discover my toxic beliefs, I could've spared myself a great deal of pain.

Now, buckle up baby! We're about to learn about toxic beliefs that are planted in childhood. Perhaps by revealing your most damaging toxic belief we can prevent you from falling into the pit of pure hell, or at least cushion the landing a bit.

Chapter 4:
What's at the Root?

Let's talk about these pesky little toxic beliefs that are inadvertently planted at a very young age. I think we can all agree that what happens in childhood doesn't stay in childhood. From the time we are born, we are learning the ways of the world from our caregivers. Unless our parents have done their own healing dance prior to us entering the world, we are likely to carry their baggage at some point in our lives. To some degree, their toxic beliefs rub off on us, sprout roots, and the cycle continues. Children are energetically sensitive, so they look to please almost immediately. From infancy we seek the approval of our caregivers because we strive to get that smile from them. We look for love, safety, and approval. This is innate. We learn quickly what pleases our parents and what they disapprove of. We know that because it either feels good or not so good. The beliefs of our parents are passed onto us at a very young age. We obtain beliefs about religion, politics, the ways in which we live, and our general culture. More important are the beliefs that are passed on unintentionally about how to view the world and our own worth. We all come out of childhood with some solid, healthy beliefs, and some harmful, toxic beliefs.

A healthy belief might be; I am lovable, I am enough, I am worthy, I am safe, or I am important. A toxic belief would be the opposite; I am not lovable, I am not enough, I am not worthy, I am not safe, or I am not important.

Knowing your core toxic belief is only the half of it. Once you uncover that little sucker, you must then understand where it came from and how it affects your current adult life. This is the only way to shift, heal, and move forward. Simply put, you need to get to the roots of that belief to make a change.

In my case, while digging to understand my core toxic belief, I came to an understanding that I put my own needs on the back burner for others continually and that brought me a great deal of heartache and pain. I had to look deep into my childhood to comprehend what it was that was missing or what was haunting me and prompting me to repeatedly make these awful choices in men. From inner child work, therapy, pages of journaling, reparenting, and the daily process I will share with you, I came to not only understand where my core belief came from, but also heal the wounds that were tethering me to this pattern in life.

I am a rescuer. There is no doubt about that. I seek to rescue those who I believe are in need. I try as hard as I can to make sure everyone else's needs are met at the sacrifice of my own. Why is that? That was the main question I had to ask myself to open the door to healing.

After turning the mirror towards myself and working my own program, I came to understand my inner voice of fear and the toxic seeds that drove that voice to consistently put me in unhealthy relationships.

In this chapter I will reveal how toxic beliefs from childhood carry into adulthood and cause havoc. Then, get ready, because in the next chapter it's time for you to face the mirror and go through the process yourself. I know from experience that can be scary, but I can assure you that it's well worth it. You want to be a hero and you want to be appreciated, so now you can have all of that by learning to love yourself and become your own hero.

Digging Deep

My mom is a bit of a perfectionist because of her own belief that she's not enough. She generally asks someone to do something and then complains about how they completed the task. I can still hear her words echoing in my head from childhood, "If you want something done right, you need to do it yourself!" Of course, this was coming from her own insecurity, but as a child you certainly don't understand that. You hear those words and think you're not good enough and nothing you ever do will please the person. I now realize that she wasn't frustrated with me, she was frustrated with life, but I was the one who spent the most time with her, so I had the honor of getting the backlash of her misery.

Important Note: Please know that if you have children and you think you're hiding your sadness, disappointment or frustration with life from them, you are sadly misled. Children are energy magnets and they 'feel' everything you are going through. We often pass our own shit onto them without even realizing it because we are reacting to life instead of responding. But that's a whole different book!

My mom is also an excellent martyr. Rescuers tend to travel the path of martyrdom when they feel unappreciated and unnoticed for their efforts. Honestly, when you're trying to rescue others and they really don't want to be rescued, it's important to note that they're not likely to be grateful.

Along with her rescuing abilities she often felt slighted and would get pissed if she felt unappreciated for her efforts. One sentence that echoes to this day in my mind and which had a profound impact on me was,

"One of these days you're going to come home and you're not going to find me!" She said this out of pure frustration and overwhelm, but again, as a young child, I interpreted this to mean that if I didn't do things the way she wanted them to be done, then she'd leave. She'd abandon me. I'm not sure she ever would've done that, but nonetheless, these statements created negative messages that played over and over in my mind until I began to pull those toxic roots from my garden of life.

I interpreted those phrases to mean that I had to please others and do what they wanted to be worthy of their love. This made me vulnerable repeatedly in relationships because I was once again not meeting my own needs but instead shelfing them for the betterment of others out of fear that they would not love me or leave me. Instances would come up in relationships and I would skirt around them or not speak my truth or dissatisfaction because I feared being abandoned. This made it difficult to be my true self because boundaries were being crossed and I was allowing that out of fear instead of speaking my truth and loving myself. There's no surprise I continually chose emotionally unavailable men to love!

Speaking of men...my father was the ultimate rescuer. He was a true fixer – always there to make things better for others. My dad was the epitome of the description of a rescuer in the introduction of this book, 'the go-to guy' who always had a plan of action. I continually looked at him as my personal hero until I felt the strain of my own cape and noticed the toll his cape had taken on him over the years. My dad never thought of himself and that prompted his exit from this life far too soon.

So, you see, both of my parents were rescuers. My mom took the route of martyrdom and was somewhat resentful, whereas my dad was the dutiful servant his whole life to his own demise. Not only was I watching rescuing unfold in front of me, but I was listening, interpreting, and processing through a toxic belief that I wasn't important.

Here's the catch...your parents aren't planting toxic seeds on purpose. They are unaware of the damage that is done because they haven't done their own healing. My mom certainly didn't understand that her words and actions were teaching me to ignore my own needs for the benefit of others, so they wouldn't abandon me. And my father wasn't thinking that by never taking care of himself he would be the perfect model for his little girl to do the same. Both of my parents felt they were protecting me and providing in the best way they could, but they had heavy baggage. Neither of them did the healing dance. They simply continued their path in life; not seeking, not digging, and not healing.

In the airport of life, when our parents have heavy baggage, we end up carrying it with them sooner or later. There is no blame here, just understanding, acceptance, and healing. I love my parents more than anything in the world. My mom is a true warrior. She has battled cancer for over 20 years and comes out smiling every damn time. I get my strength from her. My dad was a dutiful servant with a great deal of integrity and compassion. I know I learned both of those wonderful character traits from him. I have absolutely no angst towards my parents for passing on baggage – for they knew not what they did. It was their job to get me into this world and do the best they could, and they certainly did that. It is now my job to make the best of this life for myself and my son.

The Roots

When I think back to my childhood, teenage years, and early adulthood, I can certainly see how this toxic belief was validated repeatedly in all aspects of my life. Once you discover the toxic belief that is causing the most havoc, you can connect the dots among all your relationships and then begin to heal.

Imagine your life as a tree. You start as a tiny seed and then a sprout pops up and roots begin to shoot deep into the soil. The roots are the beliefs that are formed in early childhood about how the world works and what you begin to believe is true. As you grow, your trunk becomes stronger and stronger, meaning you deepen those beliefs.

This is exactly what happened in my life, your life, and every person that you know. The seed was planted, you rehearsed it repetitively, and then you manifested toxic experiences in life. For me, those toxic experiences were focused mostly on intimate relationships, but it generally doesn't stop there. There are connections everywhere in your life once you uncover your deepest toxic belief.

Giving Too Much

One of my all-time favorite books is, "The Giving Tree" by Shel Silverstein. For years, I was always drawn to that book, but I didn't understand why. I think I might know the reason now...

"The Giving Tree" is a children's book, but I firmly believe that some of the best children's books teach adult lessons if we are willing to see the lesson in front of us. This book is certainly one of those with a very deep message – especially for you, the rescuer. From one rescuer to another, I highly recommend this book as it will help you to realize how we give too much away for the benefit of others.

In this book, the tree loves a boy and continues to give and give to him throughout the entire book until the tree is no longer a tree. The tree is selfless and just wants the boy to be happy. When the boy is happy, the tree believes that it is happy, but this isn't true because the boy always leaves and then comes back wanting more.

The tree feels happy for a moment, feeling needed, and then sad again when the boy leaves. Finally, the boy makes his final exit and continues to meet his own needs and the tree is no longer a tree for it has given too much.

If you are not nourishing healthy beliefs in *your* tree of life, then you will ultimately shrivel up and die. For some, that might mean shutting down emotionally. For others, it may mean creating dis-ease within your body. And for yet another group, it may actually mean physical death. We were all given a beautiful gift at birth – the gift of life. We may not come into this world with all the same healthy beliefs, but we sure can leave this world far better than we entered – if we so desire.

We give far too much as rescuers and once we find our toxic seed that is causing havoc in our garden of life, we are free to prune the garden and enjoy the beauty of life.

I exited childhood with a toxic belief that I wasn't important and that if I didn't do what others wanted, needed, or desired, then I wouldn't secure their love and they would ultimately leave me. This was the belief I needed to focus on to heal and walk a different path.

I've talked about my childhood and where my cape first became fastened. I've also discussed my issues in adulthood related to wearing this damn cape that ultimately are tied to the childhood that created my core toxic belief. Finally, I revealed the core toxic seed that has caused havoc in my personal life. I guess you can say I've gotten a little naked here. Well, now is the time in this book for *you* to start getting naked (I mean, it's only fair).

Go to the garage or shed and get your shovel because we are about to dig deep. I've spoken of 'the garden of life' a few times and mentioned these core toxic seeds that are planted in childhood which take root like a weed in that garden. Notice I've interchanged the words 'belief' and 'seed.' That's because these beliefs that are planted during childhood are like seeds in the garden of life, and if we don't pull those suckers clear out with the root, we are shit outta luck!

In the next chapter I am going to walk you through the same process I guide my clients through. You can choose to work on this on your own, or go to the website for guidance www.vickisavini.com/member. Either way, by the end of the next chapter you should be able to at least identify the core toxic seed in your personal garden of life. This is exciting because you are getting ready for your biggest rescue ever. I hope you're ready to start digging!

Chapter 5:

Discovering Your Toxic Seed

Do you know who you are?

I'm not talking about the name you use in this life. I'm asking, do you know what makes you tick? Do you understand what drives you? Do you have any idea what keeps you going in this thing we call life? Perhaps most important; do you know the core belief that holds you back from your bliss?

In this chapter we are going to dive deep into your personal storybook and uncover the core belief that has caused havoc in your life thus far. Take a deep breath and get your shovel ready because we're about to chuck some dirt baby!

My Core Toxic Seed

You know it's in there. You sense it. You feel it. It destroys your happiness continually throughout life. You feel yourself walking this path repeatedly and somewhat unconsciously. The pain is deep, and just when you think that pain has subsided, it resurfaces with more power than ever before in a new form or relationship. When you truly desire to heal this pain, you begin to ask questions. You wonder, what is at the root of all this chaos? What prompts me to rescue others instead of taking care of myself? Why on earth can't I just lend a helping hand, but honor my own damn boundaries? Well, now you know – it's a toxic belief that is buried somewhere deep within you. So, get that shovel in hand and let's start digging to reveal your gem to *finally* heal that aching pain.

We could certainly come up with a long list of toxic beliefs that have caused havoc in our lives, but for our purposes we are going to dig deep on what I call the *core five;* I am not lovable, I am not enough, I am not worthy, I am not safe, I am not important. These are the core issues that always appear to surface early on while working with my clients and by the end of this chapter you will understand how they all boil down to one solution.

I'm going to share brief client stories to illustrate each toxic belief and where it came from. It is my hope that these stories may trigger something for you to find your own core toxic belief as I am not sitting across from you, guiding you through this journey, as I would in a 1:1 client session. Try this process and see if you're able to get to the seed on your own. If it's too difficult to do on your own I have set up resources and support on my website that will help you through the process.

Over several years of coaching, I have developed a process to help clients get to their toxic seed as quickly as possible. This is the same process I will walk you through in this chapter. When meeting with a client for the first time, I generally begin with simple questions about what they think brought them to me and what they would ideally like to shift or change. As we dialogue, a painful feeling inevitably comes up (sadness, despair, confusion, loneliness). When I see this feeling arise, I ask them to sit back and relax. I then ask my client to define the feeling in one word and tell me where they feel that in their body. We then breathe energy into that area of the body and release the tension. I do this so they can get beyond the crippling feeling of this pain and uncover what belief is tied to this feeling. I then ask them to take a few deep breaths and lead them through a simple mediation bringing them back to a point in their childhood where they felt this same exact feeling. This is the identical process you will go through. After you read the following client stories,

I will provide you with specific questions and other resources at www.vickisavini.com/member to help you through the process.

Let's get you primed and ready to dig deep for yourself by reading through a few client stories...

Sandy's Story: (I'm not lovable)

Sandy came to me just before her 40th birthday. She was on the verge of a divorce and questioning if she'd ever be truly happy in an intimate relationship with one man. Her concern was that she would never be truly happy because she found herself wandering to others even during her marriage. Her goal was to reveal what was 'wrong' with her so she could determine if she should move forward with a divorce or not.

After speaking with Sandy for just a few moments it became evident that she was a rescuer. We jumped right in with specific questions about her fears and it was swiftly revealed that there was a great deal of turmoil during her childhood.

Her parents were constantly at each other's throats. As a young child, she felt like she was always in the middle and had to call the police several times to alleviate the fighting and prevent a tragedy. When she was first recalling her childhood, she was speaking as if she were re-telling a story as a third person. Sandy said it was hard for her to *feel* her feelings and she wasn't sure she would be able to get to an actual feeling in meditation, but low and behold, she did.

We started with how she felt unloved by her husband and the things that made her feel this way. She felt that he wasn't cognizant of her needs and didn't seem to care that she was spending a great deal of time alone while he worked or did other things. She would try to tell him what she needed, and he didn't appear to do anything about it, so she got bored, needed attention and cheated but then she felt worse about herself. Through meditation we got to the root of this feeling of being unloved. We journeyed back to the first time she felt unloved in childhood, which took a little practice, but she eventually came to realize that even as an infant she did not feel loved. Her perception was that her mother was miserable and wanted nothing to do with her. During the meditation she could sense that her mother was tense even when she held her as an infant. As she grew, nothing she ever did appeared to matter. She was generally criticized for everything she said or did. She recalled being told that there was something wrong with her countless times because she was a dare devil. She would do just about anything to get her mother's attention, even get in trouble and be hit for that. By the end of our meditation, Sandy began to cry uncontrollably. I handed her a tissue and gently touched her leg to let her know that she wasn't alone. She opened her eyes, looked at me and said, "oh my God, I've *never* felt loved."

It was plain to see that her toxic belief was that she wasn't lovable, and she therefore was continually selling herself short in relationships.

Jessica's Story: (I'm not enough)

Jessica was a beautiful young woman in her late 30's. She was married with two beautiful children and she and her husband ran a successful business. From the outside looking in, one would think she had it all, but her pain told a different story.

When asked what brought her in and what she wanted to accomplish through coaching she had a very difficult time defining her goal. She talked about feeling frustrated with her career, unhappiness in relationships with both friends and family, and disappointment in her overall level of happiness. It was truly difficult for her to decipher what it was that she wanted to accomplish, but she absolutely knew that she wasn't fulfilled. We began the process together and within our first session it was clear that she had a great deal of resentment towards her parents and felt that she would never be enough.

In meditation, Jessica shared the pain of an emotionally unavailable mother who was highly critical and an avoidant father who would turn to alcohol to escape his reality. She struggled through childhood, feeling like 'the black sheep of the family' and never quite felt that she could measure up in any way, shape or form.

Shortly after college, she was on a quest to get married. Even though her husband didn't appear to want to get married, she chased after him, finally giving him an ultimatum for marriage. She had moved her whole life to open a business with him. Now, in her late 30's, she was feeling confused and wondering if this was the relationship she wanted for the rest of her life.

She didn't take much time to truly find what *she* wanted to do in life. Instead, she went along with what her husband wanted and became his partner in the business but didn't feel completely fulfilled.

In friendship, she found herself consistently frustrated with her friends who appeared to be settling in life and wouldn't listen to her advice. Jess spent all her time and energy concerned about others; what they were doing, what they were saying, how successful they were or how successful they weren't. She became consumed with the lives of everyone else around her and had no idea what she truly wanted, needed or desired.

It was crystal clear that Jessica was a rescuer and she was trying desperately to rescue her parents, friends, and husband but what she really wanted was to be rescued herself.

Jessica's toxic belief was that she was not enough. She didn't feel enough in her family, with friends, her career or with her husband. This belief came from early childhood as her mother was highly critical because she was dealing with an alcoholic husband and likely had to check out to get through her day to day routine.

Patti's Story: (I'm not worthy)

Patty came to me in her late 50's. She had been through two marriages with two different addicts and was at a point in her life where she was ready to look in the mirror. Through the coaching process it was quickly revealed that Patti's deepest core belief was *I'm not worthy*. Patti was an amazing woman who was a talented writer and creative program developer of education. She didn't take much to the finish line though and was wondering what was holding her back. She also had this tiny issue of attracting unhealthy relationships. Patty was ready to dig deep to be available for a healthy relationship and wanted more than anything to succeed in a project she was working on.

As we dialogued it became apparent that Patty's mom was highly critical of her as a child and her older sister jumped on that band wagon as well. She intensely remembered being told that she didn't know what she was talking about and to ignore her. Instead of causing turmoil or arguing, Patty took the path of what she thought was least resistant and chose to silence herself. This was showing up in her physical health as well, because she had some issues with her throat and thyroid as a result.

Patty chose unhealthy relationships because she didn't believe that she was worthy of a good man. She stopped herself from following through on projects because she questioned her abilities to the point of immobilization. Once we uncovered her toxic belief, Patty was able to heal her physical and emotional health. She became a published author and was recognized for a program she developed in education. She is also not settling when it comes to men as she finally sees her own worth and won't allow anyone to make her feel less than she knows she is.

Drew's Story: (I'm not safe)

Drew came to me in his mid-sixties. He had attended a workshop I presented on the power of affirmations and said he knew the moment I began to speak that he was supposed to work with me. Drew was a powerful man who worked for the state on addiction recovery. He was a certified MSW and ran several programs himself, yet he still felt broken and was reaching for a solution.

When we met, he shared with me that he had been through rehab several times, saw innumerable counselors and tried to work on himself for years but it always appeared like something was missing.

He felt strongly that working with me might draw him to the root.

Honestly, that was early in my coaching career and I must admit that I was feeling pressure that perhaps *I* wouldn't be good enough! Luckily, I got out of my own way and allowed the process to unfold.

Drew was sexually abused as a child by a priest and never felt safe because when he tried to go to his parents he was reprimanded and told he was lying. He learned to stuff his feelings for years until he could numb them with substances. He began smoking at 14, then began drinking shortly thereafter. The drinking led to heavy drug use and womanizing. He had quite a colorful story. In his early 30's he married and had children, but his addictions ruined any chance of happiness for himself and his family. He tried marriage a few times to no avail and finally came to an understanding that he had to heal. He ultimately abstained from his addictions but never went to the root cause until we worked together.

I still remember the look on his face when I told him his first homework assignment was to look in the mirror and say, "I love you. I truly love you. You are safe with me." After giving him the assignment, he tilted his head and then began to laugh. He asked, "Are you serious?" I replied with, "serious as a heart attack." He shook his head and said, "Ok, I'm going to try. I have nothing to lose and everything to gain."

At his next appointment he shared with me how difficult this assignment had been. The first time he looked in the mirror, he couldn't even get the words out without crying irrepressibly. He tried several times that week and was finally able to at least say the words but continued to cry. We talked about his feelings at length and why they were coming up. It was clear that he never felt safe during his childhood and put himself in unsafe situations as an adult because it was truly all that he knew. At the root, it was obvious that he didn't love himself because he blamed himself for the sexual abuse he underwent as a child.

I was so honored to work with him and see him progress through healing for himself and his children. I am pleased to say that Drew now feels safe, has developed strong relationships with his children and is enjoying life all because he dug deep, revealed his toxic seed and learned to love himself.

My Story: (I'm Not Important)

Well, I don't really think you need to hear my story again since you've heard it throughout this book, so I'll keep this short and sweet.

I spent my childhood feeling unimportant. I was the last of four children, 11 years after my third sister. My sisters had a life of their own and my mom was tired of adulting. I can remember as far back as my first few years of life standing in the playpen and watching everyone do their own thing around me. My sisters say that I got a lot of attention – and perhaps in their view, I did – but I felt that I wasn't allowed to give my opinion on anything. My thoughts and ideas were not valued and recognized because I was referred to as 'the baby.' For years my sisters or mom made decisions for me whether I asked them to or not. This coupled with the information I wrote about earlier brought me to the belief that I wasn't important and if I didn't do what others wanted me to do, then they would not love me. Thankfully, my cape is now toast and I love myself!

There is No Blame

I wanted to share one more story with you about not being enough because there's a huge connection in this story to forgiveness which is critically important in your healing process. During your healing process it's imperative not to place blame on others (parents, lovers, friends). We must come to understand that everyone is doing the best that they can. In a situation with parents, we obviously were very dependent on them for countless reasons. However, to heal, we must be able to step into their shoes to see where they were coming from and then forgive and let go. Blaming only causes resentment and ultimately takes our power away. To be clear, this is not condoning anything negative that was done to us as innocent children. Instead, it is looking back as we begin to heal as an adult and seeing the perspective of what our parents were experiencing. We do this as adults to heal our inner child and reparent ourselves.

When it comes to other adults who have caused us pain, it is also important not to focus on blaming them because as you read through my story about Richard, it wasn't until I came to understand that I was allowing this treatment of myself that I was able to cut the cord and heal.

I strive to help my clients forgive those who caused them pain, so they can truly move on with no resentment. Resentment doesn't serve us. We are all doing the best we can and when we look back at our childhood and see our parents through the eyes of an adult instead of a child, we are able to gain a different perspective and invite forgiveness into our hearts. Without forgiveness, you simply will not completely heal. As I stated earlier in the book, there is no blame.

Elaina: (I'm not enough-Forgiveness)

Elaina came to me in her late 40's. She was very frustrated with her career and questioning her second marriage. As we began our first session she cried almost immediately because she spoke of her first marriage and how she felt a doormat. This led us back to her childhood and revealed that she never felt like she had a voice, nor did she feel good enough. Her mom was an alcoholic who was highly critical and abusive to her. Every time Elaina would encounter an experience in life where she felt like she was being judged, she shut down or became defensive. This was causing problems for her in her career and relationships.

Through our work, Elaina began to heal as she found her voice and opened her heart to love herself. One night after leaving my office, her mom called. Her mom asked where she was coming from and Elaina told her that she was in counseling to heal herself. Her mom became quiet and then abruptly ended the call. A few days later Elaina received a heartfelt letter from her mom. Her mother had taken the time to apologize for her abusive nature and express concern that she was in counseling because of her actions during childhood. Her mom was 86 and asked that she forgive her before she died. Ironically, in the session prior to this we discussed forgiving her mom and why this would be important to her healing. Elaina shared with me that her mom never calls her in the evening and she was shocked to get the call after leaving this session. I smiled and said, "There's no coincidence in this Universe my dear. This is the Universe's gift to you!" Elaina's work on herself became easier as she was able to forgive her mom and stay in the present.

I wanted to share this story with you because many of my clients must learn to forgive those who hurt them through meditation because they have passed or because this person is in complete denial. It's not often that you are given this gift of apology whilst healing yourself so it's truly amazing and I couldn't help but share with you.

Ok, enough about me and my clients...now onto you!

Excavation Time!

Let's review...

You've learned all about the rescuer personality. You've identified your behaviors pertaining to that. You've learned that you're an addict because you are addicted to meeting the needs of others over yourself. You've been introduced to the idea of core toxic beliefs that were planted in childhood. You understand that what happens in childhood definitely doesn't stay in childhood, and you've heard stories of others and their personal toxic seeds. Now is the big moment, the BIG reveal. Drum roll, please!

What is your toxic seed?

You can read through this section and then walk yourself through the process, have a friend that you trust read through this and guide you, or go to www.vickisavini.com/coremeditation, click play, and I will personally guide you through. Either road you choose will get you to your core toxic seed and well on your way to healing!

The Core Five:

I'm not lovable

I'm not enough

I'm not worthy

I'm not safe

I'm not important

By now you just might have some idea of your core toxic belief, so hopefully this process will be easy for you.

Begin by reading through the list above and see if there's one that resonates more with you than any of the others. Then, sit back and relax in a chair or comfy seat. Take a deep breath in and allow yourself to clear your mind as you breathe out. Breathe in through your nose and release through your mouth. Repeat this process several times until you begin to feel relaxed in your chair.

Question 1: What is your most pressing issue? (What bothers you the most)

My most pressing issue is: _____

_____

Question 2: What aspect of your life does this issue affect the most? (Relationships, Career, Confidence, etc.)

This issue affects: _____

_____

_____
_____

Question 3: When you think about this issue, what feeling arises for you?

The feeling that arises is: _____

_____

Take a few more deep breaths to calm yourself from the feeling that is currently surfacing.

Question 4: Where do you feel this pain in your body?

_____

Breathe again, in and out.

Now that you have the feeling and you have identified where it has settled in your body, we are going to venture back to your childhood.

Breathe in and close your eyes. Breathe out focusing your breath into the pain you feel in your body. Continue to breathe in and out as you allow your body to completely relax. Imagine that you are standing at the top of a winding staircase. There are clouds all around you and the stairs are pure white. Take a step down the staircase. As you venture down the stairs imagine yourself in early adulthood.

Was there a time that you felt this feeling then?

Honor the feeling as if you are a third person watching this unfold. Do not allow yourself to attach to this feeling so that we can continue down the staircase.

Breathe in and out, releasing and relaxing your body.

Continue down the staircase. Imagine yourself as a teenager.

Was there a time when you felt this feeling here?

Honor the feeling. Breathe in and release, relax and continue down the staircase on your journey, again, detaching from the pain so that you can view this experience as if you are watching a movie.

Breathe in and out, releasing and relaxing your body.

Continue down the staircase. Imagine yourself as a child. Go to the first memory when you had this exact feeling in your childhood. Take a deep breath in. This time allow yourself to go back to that period. *Feel* the feeling. Imagine the sounds, the scents and the scenes. Who was there with you? What were they saying or doing? When the pain arises allow yourself to feel it in your body but breathe into it and release. Continue to breathe and repeat after me. I am safe. I am whole, perfect and complete. Breathe in and release out. Breathe in once more holding your breath in your lungs as if you are filling a balloon and then release and relax your body.

My deepest core belief is: _____
_____

I am not: lovable, enough, worthy, safe, important

Cue the champagne cork and let the celebration begin. You have just done some very difficult work and you are on your way to healing. You've done it. You've dug up that toxic seed. And now you might wonder, what the hell is the solution to healing my pain?

Believe it or not, that's quite simple... The solution is loving yourself and being your own hero. You can do that by committing to 30 days of self-love. Coming up next! The commitment...

Chapter 6:

A Deeper Commitment

For many years I have heard people say, 'You just need to love yourself.' I'm quite sure you've heard this a gazillion times as well. It's like a buzz phrase now. It's everywhere you go! Almost everything you read seems to follow this thought. It's in magazines, blog articles, Instagram posts, Facebook, and even music! (hint: You Should Go & Love Yourself)

'Love yourself' seems to nonchalantly roll off tongues around the world. But, seriously, does anyone specifically tell you *how* to love yourself? Is there a guide that gives you a step by step program on *how to fall in love with yourself?* I mean, it's easy to say, people, but not easy to do, especially when you've spent your whole life putting others first. You clearly have no freaking idea *how* to love yourself when you are last in line to get your needs met. That wasn't part of my curriculum growing up. You?

Guess what? Today is your lucky day because that is exactly what the rest of this book is going to teach you how to do – step by step – if you are willing and ready to commit.

If you truly want to heal and you believe that you've had enough of these toxic experiences, then *you're* going to have to change the course of your direction. You will do this by committing **30 days** to yourself. Not two or three days. Not even a week or so. You will need to commit 30 days to you, yourself, and you, to remove the toxic seed and plant healthy seeds in your garden of life.

If that seems too difficult, you're not quite sure you're ready to burn the cape just yet, or you haven't had enough pain, then you should go ahead and put this book on the shelf next to the other self-help books that you've read (because Lord knows I have quite the collection on several shelves in my home).

Self-help is an interesting concept. You see, when we are in pain or we decide we no longer want to suffer, then we attend a workshop or pick up a self-help book. When we attend a conference or workshop, we feel like we're on cloud nine while we are there. We are ready to take on the world and can't wait to get back to real life to get our shit together. Then, we generally get back to the real world and fall back into our patterns because it's what we know, and life feels too overwhelming to change. The same happens with self-help books. While we are reading them, we try our very best to change what ails us. Even after putting that book down we may have a new pattern for a short period of time. Sadly, once we think all is well, we stop working on ourselves and coast and then BAM, we're right back where we started!

I know this all too well because I personally have done this time and time again in this quest to always be my best self and find true happiness.

I'm not here to give you a temporary fix. I am writing this book to empower you to burn the damn cape and love yourself. I know this program works if you commit because I not only lived through the pain, but also learned to love myself and be my own hero in spite of that pain.

So, here's the deal put simply. If you're ready to truly shift and love yourself then you must dedicate 30 days (or maybe a few more) to yourself. You will need to commit to 30 consistent days, not only to this process but more importantly, to you. You commit to others and their well-being all the time, so I know that you *can* commit. You do not have a 'commitment issue,' so there are no excuses. I know you can do this because I did this in my darkest hour and it made all the difference in my life.

If you honestly make this commitment to yourself, I guarantee by the end of this book, you will not only be 'naked' (totally comfortable in your skin) and ready to dance in the rain, but the cape shall be toast!

You've spent a very long time snapping on that cape relentlessly trying to rescue others who honestly didn't want to be rescued. This is your chance to rescue someone who truly deserves and *wants* to be rescued – YOU. It's time to be that hero you've always dreamed of being. Get your cape out of the closet for one last gig. This is a grand rescue my friend, because this time, you will no longer feel the need to snap on your cape for others. You will have healed that desperate need to seek approval outside of yourself and you will once and for all value and love yourself. I know you don't believe it, but trust me, you **can** do this.

Please note that this shift doesn't mean you are abandoning others and being selfish. Instead, what you are learning to do is honor the giver in you but still take care of your needs, wants, and desires first. We've put ourselves on the back burner far too long. It's time to sit front and center.

It's Your Choice

It's go time. Will you put the book on the shelf or dedicate 30 days to yourself? The choice is entirely up to you. You are the captain of your ship. Either way, I support you. If you just don't think you're ready, then I thank you for reading this far, and I send you a great big hug from mi casa to your casa knowing that when the pain is deep enough and when the time is right for you, you will heal. On the flip side, if you've had enough and you are ready to learn to love yourself, then turn the page and commit.

Congratulations! You have chosen to embark upon a journey of self-love and I am so very happy for you. You will undoubtedly need your cape for the next 30 days, but the catch is that you are only allowed to use it for yourself! You must have laser focus and keep the emphasis on you. I know this will quite honestly be the most difficult part of the 30-day commitment for you. However, I am confident that if you keep the focus on yourself for 30 days, then you will absolutely change your life and never feel the need to rescue at the detriment of yourself again. *If* by chance you do, you will recognize the signs quickly and have the tools to stop yourself before going down that rabbit hole!

If you're ready to feel whole, perfect, and complete. If you're ready for the most critical rescue of your lifetime. If...you...are ready...to once and for all be your very best self then sign the following and let's get the party started!

30 Day Commitment Agreement

I _____ commit 30 days to me, myself and I. I will stay the course, read a chapter daily, and follow the exercises to the best of my ability. If that means I must wake up early or stay up late to get my general responsibilities taken care of, then so be it. If that means that I need to ask others for support to give myself the *me time* I need, then I shall ask for that as well. I will not beat myself up mentally or emotionally. I will treat myself with the gentle, loving care that I give to others. I commit to making this happen. I commit to fighting harder for myself than I've ever fought for anyone else in the past.

I am a mountain. Nothing and no-one will knock me down. I am important. I am powerful. I am worthy. I will love and protect myself like never before.

Sincerely,

_____

(Your name goes here 😊)

If you haven't done so yet, go to the closet and get your cape. Snap that baby on one last time knowing that this time it's all about you!

The next section of this book is to help you truly strip down and care for one and only person – YOU!

BONUS: You have read in a few spots of the book that there are resources available on my website to guide you (I am a teacher. I just can't help it). This is not required but simply an additional resource if you so choose.

I have designed a membership program on my site where you can click daily to get direct information on each of the exercises. If it is a meditation, then you will be guided through the meditation by my voice. If it's a worksheet, you will be given a PDF worksheet to print out. You will also be a part of a private community where you can ask questions of myself and other members and post your thoughts and ideas so that you have a new support system. There are extra video and other fun resources to help you not only look in the mirror, but love the person staring back at you. Finally, you will be part of a monthly group coaching phone call, if you choose.

You can simply read the book and do the work on your own or sign up for the membership and I will personally guide you through along with a private community for additional support.

If you are interested in this type of guidance you can check that out here:

www.vickisavini.com/member

Here is what you will need to complete the 30-day commitment to love yourself and be your own hero;

1) 30 uninterrupted days to dedicate to yourself.

2) About 20 minutes a day to read the chapter for the day.

3) The willingness to heal.

4) A journal specifically for your 30-day commitment.

PART II:
Your Journey to Self-Love

A New Day: Preparing for Your 30-Day Commitment

Whoa! That was heavy duty work you just did in the last few chapters. Good for you! You discovered your toxic seed and now you are making a 30-day commitment to yourself!

For a rescuer, it's not easy to give yourself a pat on the back and put yourself first so please take a moment and give yourself an 'atta boy or girl'. It's hard to believe that one tiny little toxic belief that is buried deep within you can cause so much turmoil, but the truth is, all it takes is a mustard seed of negativity to wreak havoc in your life.

When we come into this world we are little sponges. We take in everything around us; sights, noises, smells, and feelings. Life is like a movie that runs 24/7 for us because we are always learning about our world through what we see, hear, feel, and experience. I say 24/7 because even as we sleep, we are processing what we learned about the world in that day. We unknowingly begin this education as infants. If the same thought is validated consistently then it becomes a core belief for us.

The foundation we are given as children is critical. Of course, we are given some truly wonderful beliefs to go along with the toxic beliefs, but we all know what we tend to focus on first, don't we?

As discussed previously, you don't need to come from an awful childhood to have core toxic beliefs that hold you back in life. All you need is that mustard seed that tells you that you're not good enough, not worthy, not safe, not important, or not lovable. Ultimately, all these toxic beliefs come from fear. They come from the opposite of love and the focus is on lack instead of abundance. Over the next 30 days, you will be given tools to literally shift your negative belief into a positive future. You have given so much to others up to this point in your life. You don't have to stop being loving or giving, but you will learn to put yourself first if you follow the 30-day commitment.

During your 30-day commitment we will be creating a daily practice to incorporate into your life even beyond the 30 days. This practice will ultimately help you to keep the focus on yourself, so you can *be* your best self. Some of the exercises you do are required to continue through all 30 days. If you see this symbol ∞, note that this is a tool that will be used daily. If you do not see the symbol, then put the tool in your toolbox and use it as you see fit. Some people may want to read a chapter at night to prepare for the next day and then just re-read the exercises to complete the next morning (or throughout the day). Others may prefer to read in the morning. You will get out of the 30 days what you put into them. Remember, you are doing the rescue of a lifetime here so be steadfast, focused, and stay the course.

I'm not going to lie to you – during the next 30 days, there are going to be high waters and difficult storms to endure. You will need a quick and simple tool to keep your focus on the horizon and stay the course. Day 1 is a refocusing tool that came to me years ago. It is called the *MIRROR Process*.

I wanted to start you off with this tool on your first day because over the next 30 days, as painful feelings arise and you want to abandon ship, I want you to have this important tool in your toolbox to keep you afloat. This will be a tool that you will be able to use throughout your life to help stop negative thoughts, respond instead of reacting, and keep the focus on you.

You've done well with digging up your toxic seed in the garden of life. Now we're going to hop on a boat where you are the captain of your own ship!

Once you learn to love yourself, navigating the waters of life will be so much easier. There will still be storms to conquer, yet you will be empowered to not only survive the storm but thrive from it.

We've talked about gardens, oceans, and storms. You dug deep with your shovel to reveal your toxic seed in your personal garden of life. Now, choose a nifty toolbox because I'm about to reveal tools you won't find at the local hardware store. If you allow, these tools will empower you far beyond your imagination. I think you might just be ready for day one. Grab a journal to write about your experiences in the next 30 days and let's go forward!

***One important note that I simply must add. If you are currently in a relationship that you know is toxic – I can assure you from personal experience – that your best course of action is to step away from this person for at least 30 days. In your mind you will try to convince yourself that you can do this work while remaining in the relationship in the hopes of being stronger, honoring your boundaries, and keeping the relationship together. Trust me on this, that shit just isn't true. Been there, done that, literally wrote the book! In the grand scheme of life, 30 days is a drop in the bucket. If this relationship is meant to be, then 30 days will only strengthen it. As difficult as it may seem for you to step away from them for 30 days, please know that it is ten times more difficult to do this work on yourself while actively remaining in a toxic relationship because the focus will *never* be on you. Choose yourself this time. Remember that this critical rescue you are currently involved in is that of your own. 'Nuff said. Let's do this!

Day 1: Shifting the Focus to Me ∞

*"Self-care is not selfish. You cannot serve
from an empty vessel."*
~Eleanor Brown

Why is it so damn easy for us as rescuers to shift the entire focus of life to others? You know you do this. You spend your whole day pondering what the other person you're concerned about is thinking or feeling. You ask yourself what you could do differently to help them, make them happy, or make everything go smoother. Sadly, none of these 'critical' thoughts you're perseverating on have to do with you or what you truly need, want, or desire. Instead, it's all about the good 'ol *object of your affection*. You know, the person you're trying to please. The one you tell yourself you're trying to rescue, but you really want them to rescue you. Ah, you remember now. You get the picture.

As a rescuer, the title of day one likely makes your skin crawl. The mere thought of focusing on yourself gives you the sense that you are selfish and perhaps, dare I say, inconsiderate or mean. Allow me to give you a different perspective to ponder...

When my son was four months old we took a trip to Florida. We had to go on an airplane to get there and for the first time in all my years of traveling by aircraft I actually listened to the spiel as we were preparing for take-off. I remember it like it was yesterday.

The flight attendant began saying those infamous words, 'in the event of an emergency...' and my ears perked and tuned in. If you've never truly listened to what they are saying during this time, let me inform you that this is a vital lesson not only on an airplane, but in life. You see, the words that follow go something like this; "place the oxygen mask over your own face before securing it upon a young child or elderly passenger."

When I heard those words, my heart began to pound and my breathing increased. I went into panic thinking about an actual emergency on the plane while traveling with my infant child. My immediate thought was, 'Like hell! There's no way I would take care of myself before my child in an emergency!'

The years have shown me a different viewpoint to that phrase. Through countless trials, I have learned that if you don't put the oxygen mask on yourself first, then you might not be alive. If you're not alive, then who's going to care for those you love?

Life's experience has shown me that when I am not at my best, I am not a good mother, partner, teacher, friend, or human being. When we are depleted of joy and do not feel love, it's almost impossible to give joy and love to others. Therefore, when the focus is on someone other than ourselves for most of our day, we are not putting the oxygen mask on so that we can be our very best for those we truly love!

As a rescuer it is not easy to shift the focus from the needs of others to our own needs. Therefore, day one is a powerful 3-step process to stop the negative thoughts and shift the focus to you.

Your First Tool in Your Toolbox

When I was about 20 years old I was taking a bus from my hometown to see my sister who lived about an hour and a half away. While riding that bus I was writing in a journal about dreams I had the night before. I began scribbling the word MIRROR on a pad and couldn't quite remember why that was important from my previous night of sleep. I fell asleep once again while traveling and when I awoke I knew what it stood for; **M**y **I**dentity **R**ecognized **R**ealized and **O**penly **R**esponded to.

At the ripe 'ol age of 20, I honestly had no idea why this was coming to me and what I was to do with it, yet I knew it was significant and that I should listen carefully to this voice within. Years later while teaching a workshop it came up again and out of my mouth came the MIRROR process. Once more, I had no idea where this was going, but I knew that I should pay close attention and take notes because the Universe was delivering vital information.

I should back up a bit for you. As you have likely gathered by reading this far, I am a life coach. What you may not know is that I am an *Intuitive* Life Coach. What does that mean? It means that my coaching is powerful because I can hit upon a client's core belief within the first session since I am not analyzing them but rather listening to the voice within (a.k.a. my higher self). This powerful voice helps me to guide and coach them through healing. I have always been intuitive but just didn't understand it until my late 20's. So as much as I'd love to take credit for the MIRROR process, I can't in good faith, because I have always felt that it came *through* me and not from me. I am simply the conduit delivering the message. This process was a gift given to me from the Universe to do life changing work. I am truly honored to not only do that work on myself, but to teach you how to use this concept to shift *your* life in remarkable ways.

Not Your Typical MIRROR

The MIRROR process is based upon three major components; *Recognition, Realization and Response.* You will stand in your truth and be your true self when you use this concept to break through the barriers. The true self is the fearless being that is deep within you. The MIRROR process is a simple three step method that can be used in all aspects of life to problem solve, reduce anxiety, and tap into the power within. As you go through the next 30 days, when difficult feelings arise, reach for this tool to get you through the moment. When we are reacting to life, we are coming from a place of fear. This is when the little child within us is in charge; begging for attention; kicking and screaming. When we respond to life, we are processing differently and coming from a place of love. This is when our healthy adult is in charge. We always have a choice no matter how difficult it is to see that.

Step 1: Recognition (Awareness)

Step 2: Realization (Alternatives)

Step 3: Response (Action)

Your cape is still flowing in the breeze. You are not easily going to burn the cape and dance naked in the rain, trust me on this. In the next 30 days, as you are learning to love yourself, you are certainly going to be tested. You will want to wear the cape for others.

You will try to shift the focus to someone else. You will panic when the negative thoughts flow in. This is what the MIRROR process is for. When you find yourself in a storm of negative feelings or when you feel that you are putting the needs of others first, you must take a deep breath, step away, and process through the three steps.

The first few times you do this, it may take more than a few moments. However, I can assure you that this will become second nature the more you practice.

Ultimately, this tool will help you to get back on track and keep the focus on you when you are reacting from fear.

The Process

When a difficult feeling arises or when you begin to panic or slip into 'rescuer mode'...

Recognition – Step 1: Ask yourself, *'How does this relate to my core toxic belief about myself?'*

Realization – Step 2: *'What are the alternatives? Is this serving me or sabotaging me?'*

Response – Step 3: *'What is the best course of action that I can take to honor my own needs, wants, and desires?'*

Example 1: Let's say I am out on a date with someone new who I barely know. This person is a little touchy-

feely for me. I don't feel comfortable with this, but I don't want to hurt his feelings either because I like him enough and would like to see where things go.

Step 1: How does this relate to my core toxic belief?

This directly relates to my core toxic belief because I am allowing boundary lines to be crossed for fear that if I speak up for myself, then I am not doing what this other person wants and they may abandon me.

Step 2: What are the alternatives? Is this serving me or sabotaging me?

Alternative 1: I can continue to allow him to cross my boundaries even though it doesn't feel right to me.

This alternative is *sabotaging* me because I am inevitably teaching this person that my boundary lines don't truly exist, and their needs are more important to me than my own.

Alternative 2: I can speak my truth and tell him how this is making me feel and although I do enjoy his company, I prefer that he is not as touchy-feely on our first date.

This *serves* me for several reasons because I need to be able to speak my truth with someone I am thinking about dating. Also, if he can't respect my boundaries, then he would never be a good fit for me.

Step 3: What is the best course of action that I can take to honor my own needs, wants and desires?

The best course of action for me to honor my own needs, wants, and desires is Alternative 2.

In step one, you are simply stepping back and allowing yourself to become aware of the situation and evaluating how this relates to your core toxic belief. In step two, you must take the time to honor yourself by thinking about what is best for you. I know that's a whole new concept for you, but you will get better as you see the rewards of taking care of yourself. Finally, in step three, you act. You are no longer a victim waiting for someone else to see your feelings, meet your needs, or honor your true desires. Now, *you* are in charge and responsible for the outcome. This is not reactionary because you have become aware, looked at alternatives, and now you are ready to respond. This is the first way that we learn to love ourselves. We begin to see ourselves as important, worthy, enough, safe, and lovable.

Simply stated, the MIRROR process is a 3-step concept to help you respond to life instead of reacting to it. I am aware. I have alternatives. I respond with love for *my* highest good.

Today's Exercise

1) Say the following out loud;

Today I will keep the focus on myself. When negative feelings arise, when I begin to shift my focus to others or when I feel like abandoning ship, I will go through the 3 steps in the MIRROR process.

2) Think of an example that may throw you off during the day.

3) Fill in the steps.

Step 1: Ask yourself, *'How does this relate to my core toxic belief about myself?'*

This relates to my core toxic belief because

_____

_____

_____

Step 2: *'What are the alternatives? Is this serving me or sabotaging me?'*

Alternative 1: _____

_____

_____

_____

Is this serving me or sabotaging me?

Alternative 2: _____

_____

_____

_____

Is this serving me or sabotaging me?

Alternative 3: _____

_____

_____

_____

(Hey, you never know! You might come up with three alternatives.)

Is this serving me or sabotaging me?

Step 3: *'What is the best course of action that I can take to honor my own needs, wants and desires?'*

My best course of action is: _____

_____

_____

_____

*If you are signed up for the membership, you will find a video with more examples and a worksheet to print out under Day 1. Please go to the Facebook group (Burn the Damn Cape) to share your thoughts, struggles, triumphs, or overall experience. Community will definitely help you to feel supported and lift you up in times of need.

*The MIRROR process is an exercise that should be used throughout the 30 days and beyond to help you

keep the focus on yourself and respond to life instead of reacting to it. This is a tool to keep handy when you feel as if your focus is shifting to another person and you're turning into a rescuer once again. Keep this tool at the top of your toolbox.

Now, go have a great day with one thing in mind; the focus is on you today. Put the spotlight on yourself and just concentrate on being in the moment and use this tool as you navigate the waters of life throughout your day.

You've got this!

Lots of Love & Tons of Light,

Vicki

Journal Entry: *Journal your thoughts from today. How was your experience with the MIRROR process?*

Day 2: The Power of Affirmations ∞

*"A belief is only a thought you keep thinking
and thinking."*
~Abraham Hicks

Reminder: *When you see this symbol ∞, be advised that this is an exercise that will be used daily throughout the 30-day commitment.*

The writings of Abraham Hicks reveal that *a belief is a thought you simply keep thinking.* I remember reading those words years ago and truly allowing the message to penetrate my soul. It struck me profoundly as I realized that the thoughts I had in my mind could be projected and manifested into my life without my seal of approval if I didn't get ahold of them. You see, when the mind is in control it can take you to dangerous places, as we all know.

We live in a 'yes' Universe. Our Universe doesn't necessarily judge *what* we want. Instead, it simply provides for us.

Think of this principle as a Universal kitchen. Imagine yourself walking through the cafeteria line (you remember this from school days, right?). There you are, waiting in line, looking at all the choices before you. You look up and there's a lunch lady with that lovely hair net stretched from her forehead to the back of her neck. As you look at your choices, she quickly blurts, "You want this?" You don't even have time to think about it and before you know it, that substance, that thought, that belief is slapped onto your tray because the line needs to keep on moving.

Let me break it down even further; you think a thought, you think about it some more, you continue to think about it without even realizing it, you fear the scenario, you play out exactly what you don't want in your mind, and then BAM! You've manifested the thought into reality!

The Universe doesn't say, "Are you sure you want this?" Instead, what happens is; you think, you think again, you repeat the thought consistently and the Universe says, "Ok, here you go!" No judgement is passed. You manifest your thoughts that you've contemplated repeatedly and ultimately turn them into a belief whether you mean to or not.

Scary huh? I guess it could be. However, on the flip side, since the Universe is a 'yes' Universe and simply gives us what we ask for, then it could also be a very empowering process.

Deep inside all of us is a download that continues to play in the background as we live out our daily lives. It is literally on repeat and never stops playing. It might be; I'm not worthy, I'm not enough, I'm not important, I'm not lovable, or I'm not safe. Obviously, if we want to heal, then we must understand that this download is not the best tune for us to listen to every day. You are in luck though because you can change the song! It's time to *up*load a new playlist titled 'I love myself' with popular tunes such as; I am worthy, I am enough, I am important, I am lovable, I am safe!

The Words We Think & Speak

Let me ask you this...When you love someone, how do you talk to them? Do you belittle them? Do you find fault with them incessantly or do you lift them up with your words? Generally, when you love someone (especially when first falling in love with them) you speak kindly to them, praise them and are tender with them. You're not apt to point out their faults and scold them for making mistakes, are you? So, if we truly want to love ourselves we need to begin with the words that we say to ourselves. Rescuers are generally very hard on themselves and if we can learn to speak kindly to ourselves, then we can begin to shift from fear to love.

First, we must become a witness to the thoughts that run through our mind and the words we speak out loud about ourselves. Then, we begin to see that we may not be very loving toward that person in the mirror. For a moment, stop and think about the thoughts and words that come to mind about yourself. Generally, when I ask a client to write a list of 25 things they like about themselves, it is difficult for them to even start the list. This is because it is so hard for us to put the focus on ourselves. You learned to do that yesterday. Today, you will learn about the power of our thoughts and words.

What Are You Affirming?

Let's talk about affirmations. Did you know that an affirmation is anything that you think or say and believe to be true? Therefore, if you think, 'Life sucks and no-one truly cares about me,' then your life sucks and no-one appears to give a shit. If you think or say, 'I love life and life loves me right back,' then life is a grand ball every day of your life. We create our experiences with the words that we say or think because again *a belief is a thought we simply keep thinking.* If you want to change the tune that constantly plays in your mind, then you need to become mindful of your thoughts and words.

Of the core five toxic beliefs that I have written about, it's imperative to understand that there is only one solution; self-love. When you truly love yourself, you feel that you are enough, important, lovable, safe, and worthy. The core five are all examples of not truly loving yourself. So, let's continue the process of loving *you* with positive affirmations.

The late, great, Louise Hay taught us all that affirmations can shift your life. In her life-changing book, "You Can Heal Your Life," Louise taught us that what we give out is exactly what we get back, because the Universe totally supports us in every thought we choose to think and believe. For years I went through life thinking that I could just do a positive affirmation here and there and that my life would magically shift. That never seemed to work for me and I'm sure if you've tried it, it didn't work for you either. Then, I met Louise and saw first-hand that her thinking, in general, was full of positive thoughts. There was no let's say this affirmation once and hope it happens. She manifested a beautiful life even though she didn't love herself at one time by purely turning around negative thoughts and focusing on thinking and saying positive affirmations throughout her day-all day, every day! This is where the magic happens.

You see, we have been trained for all these years to focus on the negative and on what we do not want. Yet, the opposite is what we need to do to heal and truly love ourselves. We are energetic beings made from energy. We have our own vibration and that vibration changes based upon our thoughts. Have you ever noticed how you feel when you start thinking negative thoughts? It's not good. Your heart rate may increase, your breathing becomes shallow, and you are full of anxiety and fear, all from a thought. When we are thinking positive thoughts we feel calm, peaceful, and uplifted. We are like magnets. The more we think about something; bad, good, or indifferent, the more we draw that to us. It therefore makes sense that if we want to remove toxic seeds and replant healthy seeds, we need to be mindful of our thoughts and words.

In today's exercise, you will become a witness to your thoughts and words toward yourself and life in general. You will start your day with positive affirmations according to an intention that you will set and then you will focus on positive affirmations *throughout* your day. Notice that I did not say we are simply going to state one positive affirmation and then move on through our day. Your work today will be focusing on positive thoughts all day because it's the negative thoughts that take us down the rabbit hole in life. When we think a negative thought, we begin to focus on that thought. That thought then creates a feeling and we draw more negative thoughts toward us until we have down spiraled out of control and feel fearful, anxious, or full of despair. You do not have to spin out of control because you now have a great tool that you can use when fear raises its angry head; the MIRROR process. When the fearful thoughts creep in, use your first tool from

Day 1 to prevent you from going down the rabbit hole. The more you use it, the quicker you will turn negative thoughts around!

What's the rabbit hole you say? The rabbit hole is that place we go out of curiosity because we think we absolutely have to know the answer and we start what if-ing ourselves. We ultimately downward spiral into the bottom of a pit due to negative thoughts. Don't go there. It's not a great vacation spot or place to set up camp. Just step away from the rabbit hole.

Today's Exercise

1) Set an intention for the day.

2) Write three positive affirmations that support your intention.

3) Become a witness to your thoughts, words, and feelings.

4) Turn negative thoughts around.

5) Affirm your positive affirmations several times through the day.

6) Journal your experience in the evening.

When you rise in the morning set an intention for your day. Let this be an intention that is important to you. You may want to focus on finances, relationships, a situation at work, or your overall mood. It can be anything you would like to manifest, such as; today I am filled with joy, today I will make a positive difference at my job, today I will have pleasant conversations with everyone I cross paths with, today I will see the good in everything that happens, today I am a money magnet, or today I will speak only kind words to myself. Once you have decided what you would like to focus on; finances, career, relationships, self-love, or overall mood, then write that intention below. It is helpful to choose something that is causing turmoil for you in your life so you can begin to draw positive energy toward the situation.

Ex-1) If you are feeling like you will never find the right person in your life, your intention might be;

Today I will realize that I am lovable and worthy of a healthy relationship. I will see the possibilities in every moment.

Three positive affirmations to support this intent;

    a) **I am lovable.**

    b) **There are good people in the world looking for someone just like me.**

    c) **The right person is being drawn to me right now.**

Ex-2) If you have been feeling overwhelmed or sad, you might want to set your intention as;

Today I take life as it comes and handle one thing at a time.

Three positive affirmations to support this intent;

    a) **I am safe.**

    b) **All is well.**

    c) **I trust that everything is in Divine order.**

Today's Exercise: Your Turn

1) **My intention:**

Today I will_____

_____

_____

_____

2) **Three positive affirmations to support this intent;**

a) _____

_____

b) _____

_____

c) _____

_____

Once you set your intention and write your affirmations put them in a place where you can refer to them throughout the day because it's important to say these affirmations throughout the day as many times as you think of them (with no less than 6). Write it on a card, take a picture on your phone or carry the worksheet with you.

3) **Become a witness to your thoughts, words, and feelings.**

What does this mean? It means that you are going into a state of awareness. When you think a thought, take a moment to ask yourself if it is serving you or sabotaging you. If the thought is sabotaging you then use the MIRROR process to shift the thought and then repeat your three affirmations for the day. Notice how you feel when you are saying the positive affirmations and how you feel if a negative thought comes in. Keep in mind that the more you think a thought and feel the feeling that comes with it, the more you are drawing energy to that thought. Keep the focus on you and stay the course. If you have a weak moment, phone a friend who understands what you are doing or go to the Facebook group for support. As a witness you can stand back and look at your own thoughts so that you can offer the support to yourself that you would generally offer to someone else. Remember, you still have the cape on. This time it's for you!

4) **Turn negative thoughts around.**

If you have allowed a negative thought to come in, quickly turn that thought around by using the MIRROR process. You have this tool to use, so have at it. If you need to put a screw into the wall and the screwdriver is right there, are you going to try to screw it into the wall with your hand or use the screwdriver? Please, use the screwdriver. That's what it was made for. If you don't use your tools you lose them and ain't nobody got time for that when we're learning to love ourselves!

5) **Affirm your positive affirmations several times throughout the day.**

Some clients like to use reminders on their phone or an app that will remind them to say their affirmations. Do whatever it takes, but make sure you affirm those positive thoughts as often as possible and no less than six times throughout the day.

6) **Journal your experience in the evening.**

When you have finished your day, go ahead and journal your thoughts and ideas in your 30-day journal. Be fearless. Don't worry about what to say or how to say it, just get your thoughts and feelings onto the page. Writing is cathartic whether you think you're good at it or not. It helps us to process our thoughts and feelings in a creative and positive way.

Now, go have a great day with one thing in mind; a belief is a thought you simply keep thinking. Focus on what you truly want instead of what you do not want. When your mind shifts to fear, use the MIRROR process and don't go down the damn rabbit hole!

You've got this!

Lots of Love & Tons of Light,

Vicki

P.S. This is a tool that is used throughout the 30 days. You can choose to set a different intention daily, work with an intention for a few days until it feels like you've manifested it, r have the same intention and affirmations for 30 days. It is entirely up to you how you use this tool. Use it to your advantage to manifest your heart's desire. You're in control now. You are the captain of this ship baby!

Journal Entry: *Write about your thoughts and feelings from today. What did you notice as a witness to your thoughts?*

Day 3: Be Here Now ∞

"If you are depressed, you are living in the past. If you are anxious, you are living in the future. If you are at peace, you are living in the present."
~Lao Tzu

It's Day 3, my friends! How are you doing? I know right about this time you are wondering when it's all going to click. You might be thinking, 'I've lived this way my whole life, how the hell am I going to learn to love myself and put myself first now?' You may even be looking for excuses by now; thinking you can't keep up with the chapters – 30 days is a long time – and you're not sure you're ready. Stay the course. Keep moving through the exercises and keep the focus on you. I promise you, one day a switch goes off inside of you. For some, that switch might click on Day 3. For others, perhaps Day 10 or 12. It all depends on where you are in your healing, how bad you want to heal, and how determined you are to learn to love yourself. One thing I know for sure is that if you stay the course, that switch will most certainly click for you.

On the first day I shared the MIRROR process with you. This is an ∞ tool so you need to keep this one flowing and use it whenever negative thoughts bubble up, when you feel anxious, or when it's hard to keep the focus on yourself. It's a big, important tool in your new toolbox. The next day, you learned about affirmations and the power of your thoughts and words. This is also an ∞ tool that you need to use daily to get the true benefit. Your thoughts create your feelings and those feelings ultimately create the life that you are living.

Through the 30-day commitment you will learn to love your mind, body, and Spirit. The mind is our first barrier. This is where all the lies begin and where toxic seeds take hold. Your first group of tools focus on retraining the mind. We are going to spend a huge chunk of time here during your 30-day commitment. Today, our focus is on mindfulness. Trust the process. It was created to build your self-esteem and self-worth with building blocks that fit together ever so perfectly. I know it works because I've gone through it and I came out stronger and better than ever before. Stay with me. I know you can do the same and perhaps even better!

Mindfulness is a Life Saver

Are you mind-full or mindful? That's not a mis-spelling. There is actually a big difference. When we are mind-full our minds are full of many thoughts, worries, fears, lists, and ideas. We generally feel as if we are running on a hamster wheel. It appears our head is in a fog and we just can't seem to think straight. Nothing productive generally occurs in this state. When we are mindful, we are full of the present moment. Our mind is focused on one thing at a time and we are experiencing this moment with all our senses right here, right now. Most rescuers, amidst rescuing others, are mind-full because we are in a whirlwind of thoughts to 'save' the other person. It's imperative to understand that we are not functioning at our highest level when we are in this state.

When I was in a relationship with Richard my mind felt like it was constantly spinning. I couldn't accomplish one small task when he was around because I had so much fear and worry that I literally felt as if I was in a fog. When we were apart, you would think it would be easier to focus, but it wasn't because I spent most of my time worrying about what he was doing, who he was with, and what he was not telling me. It was an awful state of confusion and no medicine could've helped me to focus on the present moment.

I tried meditation while still in the relationship, but it was a useless effort every single time because I was full or worry, fear, and concern. More important, I was focused on him instead of myself.

I'm sure you can relate to this feeling. A feeling as if your head is in a fog. You feel as though you have a million thoughts running through your brain and you're trying to juggle ten balls in the air at the same time you're running the thoughts through your mind, all while your negative download plays repetitively in your subconscious mind. It's exhausting, isn't it?

It's a good thing you are on Day 3, because today we are going to build upon the tools you've already added to your toolbox and help to clear some of that fog away. Once we do this and you learn how to truly be mindful, you will inevitably feel a shift and begin to recognize your best self.

On Day 1, you learned to focus on yourself so there are no worries that your focus will be on someone else. Keep pulling out this tool as needed. On Day 2, you learned the power of your thoughts and words and developed a practice to set your intention and create positive experiences throughout your day. Now, on Day 3, we are going to embark upon a journey that literally gives you the room to breathe.

Today's Exercise: (If you have a subscription, you can click Day 3 for this meditation

www.vickisavini.com/member).

Sit back in a comfortable position. Put your hands on your heart. Breathe in deeply through your nose and then release slowly through your mouth. Close your eyes. Breathe in again through your nose and release through your mouth. As you breathe in, imagine the air traveling down your esophagus and into your lungs. Feel the air in your lungs and imagine it coming back up and out of your mouth. Do this several times, breathing in through your nose and out through your mouth until your body begins to relax. All you are listening to is the breath going in and out of your body. Ignore any other noises that may be occurring simultaneously. Keep the focus on your breath. Think about what it might look like, what it sounds like, and above all what it feels like. When your mind travels to other thoughts gently bring it back to the breath; listening, seeing, and feeling. Breathing in and releasing out. Repeat after me, "I am here in this moment. I am safe. I am happy. All is well." Say that three times as you breathe in and out after each sentence. Open your eyes.

Do you tell your heart to pump blood daily? Do you tell your lungs to breathe air? How about your brain? Do you tell your brain what it's function is? The answer to all the above is, no. You don't do that. You don't have to because you are always supported by the Universe whether you know that or not.

When I was a child I was a ballet dancer. I remember learning how to pirouette. My teacher taught us to focus on one point and never take our eyes off that point until we spun our head quickly and focused there again. That was the way to avoid dizziness.

This exercise will help you to refocus and avoid dizziness in life. It will keep you away from the rabbit hole and remind you that you have air in your lungs, a heart that is pumping, and a body that is functioning all without your input. Being mindful is simple. You are merely bringing yourself back to the current moment in every moment of your day. Just like you imagined what the breath looked like as it went into your body and came out of your body, and you were focused on only your breath, you will do that with everything in your day. Have laser focus. If you are having a conversation with a person, look into their eyes and listen to their words. Do not look at your phone or allow yourself to be distracted while they speak. Stay focused on them, the one person you're giving your attention to. If you are eating food, think about the food that you are putting in your body. Savor the taste and experience the enjoyment of nourishing your body. Do not rush. Take your time and allow your body to digest the food that you are giving it for sustenance. Focus only on the food that you are eating. If you are washing dishes, think only of the water, soap, and dishes in your hands. If your mind slips away to other thoughts, worries, or ideas, breathe in and release until you come back to this moment. Remember that you are always supported. Your organs are functioning without your input. Your life is evolving. Just keep bringing yourself to the present moment repeatedly. If you lose your way, put your hands on your heart and do the exercise above. Just be here now. Don't allow your mind to jump to what if and prevent your mind from getting stuck in the past. As Lao Tzu once said, "If you are depressed, you are living in the past. If you are anxious, you are living in the future. If you are at peace, you are living in the present." The present is our gift. It is all we truly have. Be here now.

This exercise is an ∞ tool. You will add this to your toolbox as part of a new daily practice. Now, go have a great day with one thing in mind; Be here now. Fear cannot and will not creep in when you are in the present moment.

You've got this!

Lots of Love & Tons of Light,

Vicki

Journal Entry: *What was different about my day when I brought myself to the present moment?*

Day 4: Mirror, Mirror on the Wall ∞

*"What matters most is how you see
yourself."*
~Louie Bryan M. Lapat

We look in the mirror daily. We brush our teeth, style our hair, or check the outfit that we are wearing in front of a mirror every day. Often when we look at the reflection in the mirror we zero in on something that doesn't look right to us or perhaps something that bothers us. The mirror generally isn't our friend, yet we're about to turn that around.

One of my best friends is a diva of all diva's. This woman just exudes confidence and sex appeal in her very essence. Andrea and I worked in a jewelry store and went out dancing on Friday nights for fun in our 20's. I would go to her house to get dressed after work and she'd inevitably change my outfit because it wasn't sexy enough (this was before I was in touch with my own inner diva). I noticed that each time before we would leave, she would look in the mirror at herself and say something like, "Damn girl, you look good," and she meant it! I wanted so badly to be able to look in the mirror and say the same thing and mean it, but I just didn't have it in me. I had just exited a relationship with a man who was older than me and had three children. I felt like a mommy before my time and Andrea noticed that. One night she stood behind me, firmly grabbed my arms and said, "Look in the mirror and tell yourself you're hot!" I started to laugh, and she said, "I'm not joking. Look in the mirror and say I'm hot!" I felt extremely uncomfortable and I barely squeaked the words out. She held me firmer and said, "Not acceptable. Say it like you mean it!" It was very difficult for me to do this because I didn't believe it at the time. She made me try again and again and I just couldn't say it and truly mean it. At one point I began to cry. She held me tightly in her arms and said, "One day, Vick, you're going to look in this mirror and see how beautiful you are. Until that day, I want you to promise me every day that you will tell yourself you're hot until you believe it." I promised her, thinking to myself that I would never do it and she'd never know anyways. Well, then my loyalty came into play and so the next day when I was getting ready for work, I tried again. It was the same. I didn't believe it, but I made a commitment to at least say the words every day, every single time I passed a mirror whether I believed it or not. At the time I was singing in a band as a side job. One night, a few weeks later, after dressing for a bar gig I stood and looked in the mirror to tell myself that I was hot. It was completely habit at this point and I didn't think the words meant anything. Yet, this night was very different. When I looked in the mirror I said, "Damn girl, you look hot," and this time I meant it! I said it again because I couldn't believe the conviction in my voice. I had a smile on my face the size of Texas and I picked up the phone to call Andrea. When she answered the phone I said, "You're not going to believe what just happened." She replied with, "Wait, did you finally believe it?" I screamed, "Yes! I believe I'm hot! I actually believe I'm hot!" She laughed and said, "Well, it's about damn time!" That experience was my very first experience looking in to a mirror and saying something positive to myself. It was the gateway to learning to love myself, but I didn't know that at the time.

The Mirror is a Powerful Tool

Every morning in my 1st grade classroom we pass around a mirror and give ourselves a compliment. Nothing makes me prouder than to hear my students say things like; I am powerful, I am amazing, I am creative, I am perfect just the way I am. My students are some of the most well-adjusted kids in 1st grade, and I have to believe it's because mirror work is a consistent part of their week. Several years ago, while teaching an empowerment camp in the summer for girls I realized the potency of mirror work. We had about 30 kids standing in front of a mirror at a dance center looking at themselves and reciting affirmations. At first, they were giggling and uncomfortable but then they became serious. At one point I said, "Ladies, stand close to the mirror and look directly in your eyes. Do not look at anyone else, only focus on your eyes. Breathe in and repeat after me, *I am important*." The room was completely silent. I asked them to say it again with conviction in their voices and realize that they are an important part of life; their words, their thoughts and their presence mattered to the world. The girls repeated, "I am important," and pure silence coupled with an undeniable energy fell upon the room. I looked at my business partner and she looked at me. We both had tears in our eyes because we knew magic just happened. Within moments I said, "Now is a good time for a snack!" As the girls fluttered around the room to sit with friends, my partner and I came together. She looked at me and said, "Did you feel that?" I replied, "I sure wish someone taught me that at 7 years old."

Magic. It was pure magic because in that moment, girls ages 7-12 understood that they mattered. Imagine if we all felt that we were important, every...single...day.

Beginning to Truly See Yourself

You know what normally happens when you look in a mirror. You look at yourself and inevitably find fault with something. It's far and few between that you can look in that mirror and like the person staring back at you. Allow me to teach you how to not only like that person but love that person with every fiber of your being. You do realize by this point that you need to fall in love with yourself before you can rip the toxic seed out of your garden of life and replant beautiful seeds, right? Then let's think about this logically. Generally, when we fall in love with someone we like what we see. We could stare into their eyes for hours and we are happy to give them compliment after compliment. We become enamored with not only what we see but also all the possibilities of them. Well, now it's time for you to turn the mirror in your direction and create those same feelings.

Today's Exercise:

Stand in front of a mirror in a private space and say this phrase, "*I love you. I truly love you. I accept you and love you for exactly who you are in this moment.*"

I'm not going to tell you that this is going to be easy the first time you try. Truth is, it's going to be hard, really freaking hard. I also know that once you do this on a regular basis you will feel unbelievable strength from this simple exercise.

Next, you're going to take the three affirmations that you have for the day (from Day 2 where you set your intention) and look in the mirror and say those affirmations. This is going to make those affirmations so much more powerful because now you are accountable to yourself. It's empowering. Trust me. I know it sounds a bit crazy or woo woo, as some might say, but do it and don't judge because you will see amazing results.

I do this same activity every morning so when you're doing this activity and you're feeling foolish, I want you to think, 'Vicki is doing this same activity right now with me.' We will get through this together, all of us.

Mirror work is important to do every morning to set the tone of your day, but you must be consistent. This is an ∞ tool so it becomes part of your daily practice. You now have four tools to practice daily and I know it may seem like a lot, but this is what is helping you to put yourself first and learn to love yourself, so stick with it.

I also use mirror work if I am feeling insecure about something. I go to the mirror and say the opposite of what I am thinking. Ex) If I am preparing a video and I'm feeling nervous, my fear driven voice might be saying, 'Who do you think you are?' I turn to the voice of love and simply walk to a mirror and give myself a pep talk. I might say, "You have a gift to give the world. You are a powerful public speaker and what is meant to come from you will effortlessly flow from you today." If that doesn't make me feel better, then I keep going until I'm ready for the presentation. I almost always say, "I love you Vicki. I truly love you." I say this because we always need to know that we are loved and that someone has our back, and now I know that I am that one person I can always count on. Soon, you will too!

Important Note: *I want you to understand that all these exercises I'm sharing with you are to build a practice for you so that you can fuel your tank with love and acceptance. If you were a car, you would need gas to keep going. If you don't put gas in, you would break down on the side of the road. It's the same for you and me. We need to fuel ourselves so that we can keep going. You can't run on an empty tank. You need to fuel yourself with positive energy. These tools will help you to do so proactively.*

Recap of Today's Exercise:

1) Go to the mirror in the morning and say, "*I love you. I truly love you. I accept you for exactly who you are in this moment.*"

2) Repeat that statement a few times and really allow it to seep into your soul. Cry if you must. There's no harm in doing so. You have a right to shed a tear or two (or hundreds). You may cry today or for several days, but there will come a day when you no longer cry, and you instead embrace and believe these words.

3) Say the three affirmations you have planned for the day that relate to the intention you've set.

Now, go have a great day with one thing in mind; love that person staring back at you when you look in the mirror.

You've got this!

Lots of Love & Tons of Light,

Vicki

Journal Entry: What was the hardest part of doing mirror work for you? How did it feel to compliment yourself while looking into your own eyes?

Day 5: Perspective Shift ∞

"If you realized how powerful your thoughts are, you'd never think a negative thought again."

~Peace Pilgrim

In 2009 I lost the one man who I honestly consider a man of integrity and my rock in this life. My dad was an amazing man who was the best damn rescuer I ever did see – I learned from the best! I felt devastated from the loss of my dad for many reasons, but mostly because he was the only one I felt I could talk to who understood me and knew what to say to get me back on track even if there were no words spoken. I was dangerously close to the edge emotionally following his passing. I cried every day and every night because I just didn't know how to cope. It took months for me to limit my crying to just the evenings and finally stop altogether with only a few tear ups throughout a day. The crying stopped but I was left feeling cheated, abandoned, and very negative. I worked hard to turn my negative thoughts around and honestly felt that I was a very positive person by mid-2010 when my children's book was released. Nevertheless, the Universe was getting ready to teach me an important lesson (gotta love how the Universe does this when you least expect it).

I came across an article that stated roughly 80-90% of our thoughts are negative. I figured that was true for me in the previous year due to the loss of my dad, but I now felt that I had shifted and was a more positive person. I also couldn't imagine that this was true for a clear majority of the population. I decided to have fun with it. I grabbed a tiny notebook and wrote tally marks for all the negative comments I heard, thought, or said in a day. Holy shit! By the middle of the day, I felt like I was weighted down with all the negativity! That's when I developed the 80:20 rule. It is your next tool to truly love yourself.

I found by focusing on the negativity I was able to realize why most people feel drained by mid-day. Negative thoughts cause worry, stress, and fear and I think we all know that doesn't feel good. As a rescuer, it's ten times worse for you because you are highly sensitive, and you are a problem solver who can't stand to leave a stone unturned. This is an ∞ tool. It's not added to a morning routine, but it is important to keep the focus on what really matters. I encourage you to use this tool as often as necessary to fuel your tank with that positive energy discussed previously.

The 80:20 Rule, Short & Sweet

After reading the article and executing my little experiment I was determined to flip this around. I felt that if 80% of our thoughts were negative and 20% were positive, then we could certainly flip this to go in the opposite direction if we were mindful and somewhat protective of our thoughts. I decided that from that point forward I was going to focus on only allowing 20% of my thoughts to be negative. The other 80% of my thoughts would be focused on positive energy (notice how the MIRROR process and daily affirmations will come in handy here).

For this exercise, you will need to be a witness to your thoughts once again (Yes, we're still focusing on the mind. Lots of training to happen here to love yourself and be your own hero). Every time I thought a negative thought, I would stop myself and ask if this was worth my 20%. I literally counted the hours in the day and knew how many hours I could technically be negative compared to the hours I had to be positive. Whenever a negative thought would come up, I would ask myself, "Is this really worth my 20%?" I became somewhat stingy because I knew I only had 20% to give to negative thoughts so I didn't want to sweat the small stuff. What I learned from this was that I was so focused on not giving attention to small negative thoughts that those thoughts didn't have time to manifest into anything worth thinking about. Before I knew it, I was thinking positively 90% of the time and only negative when I deemed it absolutely necessary – after all, we all need a little bitch time!

Let's say that you wake around 6am daily and you go to sleep by 10pm. That gives you about 16 hours a day of awake time. If you follow the 80:20 rule, then that would mean that you are allowed 3.2 hours of negative thoughts. That breaks down to about 11 minutes per hour. As you can see, you really don't get much negative time. So, if you have something that's really pissing you off or making you feel sad, then you might want to use the 20% for that. If your negative thoughts aren't so important, such as; I always get the red lights, the weather is terrible today, or dating really sucks, then you should release those thoughts as quickly as possible, so they don't take up your 20%.

This exercise is ultimately another way of helping you to shift your thoughts knowing that what we think about, we bring about! Ready for your day?

Recap: By this point in your 30-day journey you have five ∞ tools;

1) Day 1: **The MIRROR Process**...Take a step back, become aware, look at alternatives, and then take action. Use this tool as needed on a daily basis.

2) Day 2: **Intention/Affirmation**...Set that intention daily and have 3 affirmations to say throughout the day to affirm your intention. Continue with this through the 30 days. Remember it can be the same intention and affirmations or different, but you must be consistent.

3) Day 3: **Be Here Now**...Bring yourself back to the current moment throughout your day. Remember to keep the focus on the moment you are in because when we are stuck in the past we may be depressed and when we are thinking of the future, we can become anxious. Be here now.

4) Day 4: **Mirror Work**...It may seem like this little tool is silly or of little necessity but believe me, this is the tool that will change your life in ways you cannot imagine. Keep looking in that mirror and speaking words of love and positive affirmations to the person staring back at you. Remember, we are falling in love with that person, so be kind.

5) Day 5 (today): **The 80:20 Rule**!

As you can see, some of these tools will become part of a morning practice (i.e. intention/affirmations and mirror work). Others will become a shift in perspective that you will rely on throughout your day (The MIRROR Process, Be Here Now and the 80:20 Rule). It's exciting to have all of these new tools for your toolbox, right?

Today's Exercise:

1) Be a witness to your thoughts.

2) Break down approximately how many minutes you have per hour to be 'negative' (or use my equation – whatever floats your boat).

3) When negative thoughts come in; stop, breathe, and ask yourself if this thought is really worth your 20%. If it's something that you honestly feel needs your attention right at this moment, then by all means take that 20% and problem solve for yourself. If it's really not that important and just sabotaging you, then let it go and use your other tools you've been given so far to keep the focus on you.

Go ahead and use this philosophy throughout your day so that you will keep yourself away from that damn rabbit hole. By focusing on the positive and releasing useless negative thoughts, you will free your mind and enable yourself to do some solid problem solving for yourself.

Now, go have a great day with one thing in mind; you are only allowed 20% of your time to be negative. Be stingy.

You've got this!

Lots of Love & Tons of Light,

Vicki

Journal Entry: *What were the challenges I faced today in flipping my thoughts around? How did I feel overall during my day? At the end of the day, what am I feeling?*

Day 6: I Can See Clearly Now

*"Once you see someone for who they really
are, you can't go back to seeing them for
who you thought they were."*
~Tara Geraghty

We all wear masks and we all idealize people because
we want so badly to create the happiness in our
reality that we envision in our minds. One of the most
powerful lessons I learned in the process of loving
myself was that I needed to *see people for who they
are, not who I want them to be.* As rescuers we always
see the best in everyone we meet. We look beyond
the flaws, red flags, and blatant warning signs. We look
deep into their hearts and see the light within them.
When we see the broken pieces, we immediately
want to put those pieces back together for them even
though we have no idea how their puzzle connects.
Perhaps it's because we are very loving people and we
want to give everyone the benefit of the doubt. Maybe
it has something to do with wanting to be the hero, or

possibly it goes back to needing that guarantee that they'll never leave because we made such a difference in their lives. I'm not sure. However, what I am implicitly sure of, is that when we don't see people for who they are, we only end up disappointing ourselves.

Rescuers measure everyone up to *their* standards, whether we care to admit that or not. You know how you would treat someone or what you would do for them, so you expect that to be reciprocated. Truth is, what we will do for others isn't always healthy. Sometimes, what we offer isn't healthy because we put the needs, wants, and desires of other people in front of our own. This is ultimately the detriment of our own health and self-worth. As discussed in the beginning of this book, we do this because of our deep need to save someone or something and feel valued. This all goes back to our toxic core belief and once we heal that, we no longer sit in the backseat. Knowing that my toxic core belief is *I'm not important* empowers me to see how that ridiculous belief can lead me down a road of pain, time and time again, if allowed. When we don't feel important, we shrink from the amazing person we truly are to a tiny shell. Think of your toxic belief for a moment and contemplate how this belief has held you in relationships or situations that were not serving you.

Today, it's easy to idealize people and relationships. Look at 'Fakebook.' People scroll through social media thinking that everyone else's life is perfect; 'Look at that couple, they look so happy.' 'Awe, look at them, taking all those family vacations.' 'Wow, his business is so successful!' Truth is, it's all marketing. We are all marketing ourselves daily. Putting the mask on and posting that out to the world. Most people realize that social media is kind of like Hollywood. It's not what it appears to be. However, rescuers not only idealize others, but they keep trying to make that person turn into the person they once thought they were until it drains the life out of them.

It's time to go to 'Realville.' If you want to see a person's true colors, you need to stand back, watch their actions instead of listening to their words, and get real with yourself. Words will not always give you an honest picture of who a person really is, but their actions will. When their actions show you that they are not the person you imagine or who they profess to be, then it's time to protect yourself, be real, and make choices to serve you.

It's important not to judge here. Just accept the people in front of you for who they are and stop expecting them to be who you want them to be. When we get real, we draw boundary lines and we no longer allow people to cross them. That sometimes means we need to change the relationship or step away. This is a huge part of loving yourself because staying in any kind of toxic relationship is a betrayal to you and only you.

Friendship

I know who you are. You are that person who thrives on solving other people's problems. You like to help people to 'see the light' and be their very best. If you don't have the answer to their problem, you will seek and find one ASAP! You're a good friend. You are there for friends no matter what, yet you might feel frustrated because that's not always reciprocated. You're the strong one. You're the one who keeps on keepin' on. You've gone through hell and back and you're still standing. Your friends have come to understand that they can count on you. Maybe you're a lucky one. Perhaps you have a few friends that you can count on in the same way that they can count on you. Amen! Thank your lucky stars! The other friends; see them for who they are. If they aren't there for you when you really need them, then it's not a bad idea to step back and refrain from offering solutions to *their* problems. This isn't selfish. It's self-care. See your friends for who they are; the goodtime pal, the quiet evening friend, the deep intimate conversation bud, the casual diner, the hello neighbor, or your bestie. Know that not all your friends can reciprocate the same level of assistance as you can, and just accept them where they are. If you need to fill a category and you don't have a friend for that, then go out and make a new friend in that venue. There are billions of people in this world, give someone a chance to be the friend you need in that category instead of trying to force another friend to be something that they are not.

If by chance you have a friend that is toxic, you need to ask yourself if you are serving or sabotaging yourself by remaining in this relationship. Friends shouldn't drain you. You may be able to change the relationship by pulling back your level of support and problem solving to create distance. However, if that doesn't work, no matter how loyal you are, you need to take care of you. Again, always ask; *am I serving or sabotaging myself*? You might be afraid of betraying someone else whom you feel is toxic, but when we truly love ourselves, the person we don't ever want to betray is the person in the mirror.

Family

I'm the weird one. I'm the one who's interested in different religions, tarot cards, crystals, sweat lodges, and Spiritual retreats! I was always the 'odd one out' with my family. I stopped years ago trying to fit in with them. It just became too painful to keep trying to fit a hexagon into a square! I still love them and appreciate them for who they are, but ya know, we're never going on a Spiritual retreat together and that's OK by me. You are who you are. Love that. Embrace that. Be all of that! Your family may or may not 'get you.' Eh, it's not that important. We don't need their approval. Remember, 'what matters most is how *you* see yourself.' You may have completely different philosophies of life with your family members or at least one. It's doesn't mean that you stop being family. Instead, see them for who they are with no judgement and stand tall and firm in who you are. No-one needs to cross to the other side. I see you, I love you, I accept you from over here.

Now, perhaps there is a toxic relationship within your family; a narcissist, an addict, a drama queen, a martyr, or an energy vampire. You are related to them and you may have a great deal of contact with them, but once again, remember serving or sabotaging? No matter what kind of 'ship' you are in, it's important to remember that the one person you will no longer betray is yourself. This sadly may lead you to distance yourself from family members or sever your ties altogether. It's not the end of the world. Distance can be very healthy and what's most important is you creating boundaries and not allowing them to be crossed.

Intimate Relationships

Most or our arguments in a relationship begin with wanting something from another person that they either do not want to give or cannot give. In an intimate relationship, just like any other relationship, you get a choice; serve yourself or sabotage yourself.

Toxic Relationship: If a person presents themselves one way to you when you first come together, and that person quickly disappears, then you can be sure that true colors are shining through. Don't wait around for this person to magically turn into the person they advertised to you. See them for who they are in the moment. If that person isn't what you truly want, need, and desire, then get the hell out as early as possible. Remember my rock bottom? Dick showed me and told me who he truly was in week three! I chose to turn the other way, make excuses, and doubt myself instead of him. Bad choice on my part. If it looks like an orange, smells like an orange and tastes like an orange, it's an orange! Lose the cape. You're NOT going to fix them, heal them, or change them. Fix yourself, heal yourself, change yourself. Then you won't ever be in a toxic relationship again. You get the choice to save yourself and walk away or betray yourself and stay. It's honestly up to you.

Healthy Relationship: We generally come together in relationships because we are not carbon copies of one another. There is no relationship that doesn't pose challenges and that's fine because we grow from the challenges in life. If you're lucky enough to be in a relationship that is supportive and soothing to your soul, then your choice is a little easier. You simply must learn how to communicate with your mate and learn what your non-negotiables are. If it bothers you that they are slobs, then give them one room or area in the house that's just theirs and the rest of the house needs to be kept neat. If they have a strange habit or hobby, find a way to make it a win-win situation. However, if there is something that crosses a boundary line for you, then you need to serve yourself by standing your ground and discussing your concern without caving (as rescuers normally do). Look for the win-win where there is an actual compromise. In a healthy relationship, this isn't difficult because both parties involved *want* to support one another.

Today's Exercise:

1) Today you will take off the rose-colored glasses and become an observer with your 'ships' (relationships).

2) When the sensation arises, and you want to jump in and solve a problem for someone else, stop and ask yourself if you are serving or sabotaging yourself.

3) Look at your 'ships' differently today. View your friends, lovers, and family in a different light. See them for who they are instead of who you want them to be. Instead of being 'reactive' in relationships where you do not feel your needs are fully met, step back, breathe, and see the person for who they are.

4) Begin to think about boundaries; what boundaries you currently have, what boundaries have been crossed, and what boundaries you need. *Hint:* Tomorrow's exercise focuses on boundaries ▯

Now, go have a great day with one thing in mind; see people for who they are, not who you want them to be.

You've got this!

Lots of Love & Tons of Light,

Vicki

Journal Entry: *What boundaries do you currently have? What boundaries do you allow others to cross? What boundaries do you think you may need to honor to truly love yourself?*

Membership Preview: If you have signed up for the 30-day subscription, today you will find a nifty video that explores relationships in more detail along with tools to distance yourself when needed.

www.vickisavini.com/member

Day 7: Say What You Mean, Mean What You Say

"Daring to set boundaries is about having the courage to love ourselves even when we risk disappointing others."
~Brene Brown

You know what isn't good for you. You're very clear on what doesn't feel right and what you need to feel safe, happy, and peaceful. Yet, somehow, you will put yourself in awful situations to avoid disappointing others. It's who you are. You're a rescuer. This is what you do. You problem solve, smooth things out, and clear the path for all of those around you. You set boundaries with the intent of taking care of your own needs, but if you fear that you'll disappoint someone, you allow your boundary lines to get crushed to avoid conflict. You're strong. You can handle it. The other person really needs your support and understanding.

Bullshit! It's time to set boundaries to take care of ourselves and stick with them even when other people are disgruntled by them. You remember that cape that's around your neck? Let us recall that this is your last 'official' rescue. It's time to save yourself. Intact, honored boundaries are a necessity, not a nicety!

Setting Healthy Boundaries

What is a boundary anyways? A boundary is an imaginary line in our minds that tells us what we are willing to deal with and what is non-negotiable. Boundaries are not only essential for healthy relationships, but they are essential for a healthy life in general. We need these lines to protect ourselves from feeling hurt, overwhelmed, or taken advantage of. Rescuers generally don't set many boundaries and when they do set boundaries, they don't often honor them in fear of upsetting another person. That all needs to change for you to have a healthy relationship, not only with others, but with yourself. Setting healthy boundaries and honoring them is easy. However, there are a few rules that you may not know.

Setting Healthy Boundaries for People in Your Life

Rule 1: *Set boundaries that serve you, not sabotage you.*

Sometimes, we set boundaries to scare another person into doing what we want them to do. We propose a boundary and a consequence, but we really have no intention of following through with the consequence because our fear of losing them outweighs our fear of betraying ourselves. It all goes back to *'seeing someone for who they are instead of who we want them to be.'* If you are only setting a boundary to coax someone into doing what you want them to do (even if it's what you believe is best for them), then it's not a true boundary. Instead, that is manipulation. This will never serve you or the other person. It may start with a good intention, but if you're not truly going to follow through, it's just a sad attempt to make them change. No-one wins here.

Rule 2: *Be clear and concise about your expectations and consequences for crossing the boundary.*

When you set a boundary with a person, it is important to let them know ahead of time so that they can avoid crossing that line. If you keep this in your head, then you are sabotaging yourself and the other person because it is unfair to assume that they will read your mind. Set boundaries and put signs on the front lawn that they exist! People cannot honor your boundaries, unless they know they exist.

Rule 3: *Say what you mean, mean what you say.*

This one is simple; don't say it's a boundary if it's just a wish. If you are setting a boundary and you give a consequence, then you must follow through. If you want people to take you seriously and respect you, then you must respect yourself. You need to say what you mean and mean what you say. Otherwise, there's no sense in even setting a boundary.

Example for a Parent:

Let's say that your child is begging for a cell phone. You tell them that you have no problem getting a cell phone for them so that you can be in touch with them and be sure they are always safe. The one requirement you have is that they need to text you back within a few minutes when you text and they need to pick up their phone when you call, otherwise, they will lose the privilege of the phone. Be sure that you've set clear boundaries and that your child completely understands what is expected. If your child ignores your text messages and doesn't pick up the phone, they've crossed a boundary line.

Bear in mind that you must always get to the root to find out why your boundary was crossed. Perhaps the phone was not receiving text messages for some reason or the ringer was off and they didn't hear the phone. The first time that happens, you problem solve. You might say, 'I understand you weren't getting my messages. When you're away from the house, I need you to check in with me every hour,' or 'from now on, when you are away from the house, please be sure your ringer is on.' After you problem solve, if this continues to happen, then it is obvious that they are crossing your boundary line intentionally and you need to follow through with your proposed consequence.

If you do not take the phone away, then you've just allowed them to cross that boundary without consequence. More important, you've just taught them that your boundary lines don't really matter because there's no follow-through. They therefore won't take your boundaries very seriously. This might frustrate you because you feel as if they are walking all over you. However, they are not to blame. The person you need to look at is yourself. People will only cross our boundary lines if allowed.

Example in a Relationship:

Picture this...you are in a romantic relationship with someone who isn't always considerate of your time. You are living together. You cook dinner expecting them to be home by 6 pm and they don't show and don't call. You text them to see what is going on and you don't hear from them for hours. Around 9 pm, they send a text message stating that they are out drinking with friends and not to worry but when you try to call, they will not pick up the phone. You are upset and tired, so you try to go to bed. You toss and turn for a bit and then finally fall asleep only to be awakened at 2 am because they now need a ride home! Set a boundary that serves you, be clear and follow through.

"I didn't appreciate you not calling last night when you specifically told me you would be home at 6. I had dinner ready and was waiting. I also didn't appreciate you staying out until 2 am and then waking me up to pick you up because you were irresponsible and drunk. In the future, if you say you're coming home at a certain time, call me ahead to let me know that has changed. Also, if you continue to disregard me and be inconsiderate, I will no longer be in this relationship."

Setting boundaries may be all new to you or may be somewhat difficult. It's OK to admit that this has been a struggle in the past. Now, you have a few rules in place and you will be able to set healthy boundaries for yourself, giving clear expectations and consequences. You know what is right for you. You know what feels right and gives you peace of mind. You are therefore the only one who can protect yourself from feeling hurt. Set the boundaries, be clear, and follow through. It will change your world!

Today's Exercise:

Today, you will choose one aspect of your life where you need to set a boundary. Fill out the following and go forward with your day. If you need help, check out the video on the membership page or check in to the private Facebook page.

Rule 1: Set boundaries that serve you.

Be sure you are setting a boundary that you will follow through with. Remember, people will only cross your boundaries if you allow them. Also keep in mind that if you want to be respected, you must respect yourself.

What do you need to feel safe, secure, and peaceful?

Boundary: _____

_____

_____

_____

_____

_____

_____

_____

_____

_____

_____

_____

Rule 2: Be clear and concise about your expectations and consequences for crossing the boundary.

No beating around the bush here. Say what you need and what will happen if that boundary is crossed.

I expect _____

_____

_____

It's important to me because _____

_____

_____

If the boundary is crossed _____

_____

_____

Rule 3: Say what you mean, mean what you mean.

Go back and review your boundary, expectations, and consequence because if you're not able to follow through with the consequence, then it's not truly a boundary. We're aiming for respect here. Respect yourself and others will begin to respect you and your boundaries!

Now, go have a great day with one thing in mind; say what you mean, mean what you say.

You've got this!

Lots of Love & Tons of Light,

Vicki

Journal Entry: *What are the fears I feel around setting boundaries? How does it feel to set a boundary that is clear, concise and has consequences for crossing it? How will I ensure that **I** will honor my boundaries?*

Day 8: The Power of Forgiveness

"Forgiveness is the gift you give yourself."
~Suzanne Somers

Forgive and forget. Forgive, but don't ever forget. Forgive with all your heart. Forgive, but protect your heart. I'm sure you've heard all the sayings about forgiveness and you've tried countless times to forgive others when you have felt hurt or betrayed, but this can be a difficult task. You've been hurt repeatedly in your life. You've felt betrayed and beaten down and you've often wondered why you are treated this way. The truth is, it's not about forgiving others. Instead, the forgiveness we need to focus on as rescuers, is forgiving ourselves.

I once had a client say to me that forgiveness is difficult for her because she felt as if the same scenarios continued to happen repeatedly in her life. I smiled and asked why she thought that was occurring. She tilted her head, looking kind of confused, and I sat back and waited. The lightbulb went on and then she said, "Oh! I keep doing the same things repeatedly with different people and I'm expecting a different result!" Bingo! Much of this goes back to what you learned on Day 7. When we set boundaries, we need to make sure we are serving ourselves, being clear, and following through with the consequence if the boundary is crossed.

There will be plenty of times when someone crosses a boundary of yours and they are apologetic. Unfortunately, there will be more times when boundary lines are crossed and there is no apology. This is another time to be real with ourselves. We need to come to an understanding that people only cross our boundaries and continue to do so if we allow them to. We should also understand that most often, people are not intentionally trying to cross our boundaries or hurt us (that happens, but it's far and few between). Instead, people are simply looking to get their immediate needs met and are not necessarily thinking about how that affects you. This is why it's critically important for us – as rescuers – to learn to love and protect ourselves.

When I was dating Richard, there were several boundary lines crossed. When I would try to talk to him about crossing my boundary lines, he would turn it around on me and manipulate the conversation. I would walk away feeling completely drained and unsure of what just happened. Each time a conversation happened like this, I would give him the benefit of the doubt instead of trusting my own intuition. You absolutely know when a boundary line has been crossed, whether the offending party admits it, or not. It's your choice to follow through with a consequence. I sadly made huge mistakes in that relationship because I ultimately taught him that it was acceptable to cross my boundary lines. I didn't follow through with a consequence due to my own fears and that led to a lack of respect. It's a damn good thing those days are over!

Forgiving; Remorse, No Remorse, Past Hurt, Present Hurt

Often, people are unaware that they have hurt you in some way. You have an agenda and they have a separate agenda. It's not about hurting you on purpose. Instead, it's more about them taking care of themselves. If you have followed the rules from Day 7 in setting your boundaries and the other person is truly apologetic, then forgive them and move on. Dig deep as you ponder the situation and ask yourself if you were seeing them for who they truly are or for what you wanted them to be. Most of the time, we are placing our own expectations on others unknowingly. This again is because we expect that people are going to treat us the way we treat them, and that's just not always going to happen.

More often you will have to forgive someone without an apology. This is difficult because you feel wronged and betrayed. You believe that their apology will make the situation better, but it won't. The apology isn't what makes the situation better. What eases the pain is you coming to an understanding that you were hurt because you somehow betrayed yourself. Try not to have expectations of others. Don't expect them to succeed and don't expect them to fail. Instead, focus on what *you* need in the situation and what *your* boundary line is. You are responsible for you and only you. You have no control over others, but you do have control over yourself. It is you that you need to forgive for putting yourself last. The most powerful type of forgiveness that you will ever experience is that of forgiving yourself.

The only way to truly forgive is to put yourself in someone else's shoes. When I am working with clients we work hard to forgive parents or caregivers from early childhood. Clients are not able to do that until we can shift the perspective, remove them from the equation, and look at their childhood like a third person. Once they step back, they can see their parents as human beings on this journey called life, instead of the caregiver who damaged them in some way. We look at what their parents were going through as adults and how they were doing the best they could with what they had to offer during that time. We also discuss the childhood that their parents had to gain insight into *their* toxic beliefs. This doesn't make it excusable if you were harmed as a child in some way, but it sheds light on the situation and helps us to release resentment. We then understand that our parents had pain that they too were dealing with, yet they didn't do the healing dance that you are doing today and so they passed that pain on to you. We can then forgive them for *they knew not what they did* due to their own childhood experiences and hardships and begin to re-parent ourselves (as you are technically doing now in this 30-day commitment).

The definition for the word forgive is to stop feeling angry or resentful toward someone for an offense, flaw or mistake. If you want to stop feeling angry or carrying resentment, then you will need to forgive yourself. People have taken advantage. They've annihilated your boundaries, but that was before you knew the rules of boundaries and the importance of loving you. You're on a different path now. You no longer have to wait for someone else to notice that you are lovable, worthy, enough, safe, or important. Now, you've got someone who always has your back-YOU!

Today's exercise is about forgiving yourself for self-betrayal by not putting your needs, wants, and desires first.

Today's Exercise: (you may want to answer the following questions in your journal)

A betrayal that sticks in my mind is: _____

_____

_____

_____

_____

_____

Did I have clear boundaries there? _____

_____

Did I allow my boundary lines to be overstepped?

_____

What could I have done differently? _____

_____

_____

_____

_____

_____

Meditation: (Record this on a voice memo of some sort to play back to yourself, have someone read this to you or – if you are a member – go to the membership site and click Day 8)

Sit in a comfortable spot or lay down on the floor, couch, or bed. Take a deep breath in through your nose and gently release it through your mouth. Close your eyes. Breathe in again through your nose and release through your mouth. Allow your body to relax. Take a third breath in and imagine a beautiful white light just above your forehead shining brightly. Breathe out and feel that warmth of the light on your head like sunshine on a warm summer day. Breathe in and imagine that light traveling down over your face and around your neck. Breathe out and see the light travel into your heart. As the light circles your heart, imagine that you are walking down a staircase. Continue to breathe in and out. Focus on your steps as you walk down each of the stairs in front of you. Imagine yourself going back to a time in your childhood. The moment you envision yourself as a small child, go to that child, pick them up and hold them tightly. Let that child know that they are loved and safe with you. Whatever your toxic core belief is, tell your inner child (this child you are embracing) the opposite of the negative belief. You are loved. You are safe. You are important. You are worthy. You are enough. Hold them tightly and feel the love in the embrace. Imagine that child snuggling up close and whispering in your ear, "I forgive you. Thank you for taking care of me. I love you." Breathe in through your nose. Release out through your mouth slowly. Continue to breathe in and out as you walk back up the steps with this child, your little self, holding tightly to this important child. Feel the love. Just feel the love. Know now that you will never betray yourself again. You will always protect your heart. You will set clear boundaries that serve you and follow through with consequences because you are protecting the child within.

Now, go have a great day with one thing in mind; protect and love the child within always. Forgive yourself and never abandon them again.

You've got this!

Lots of Love & Tons of Light,

Vicki

Journal Entry: Tonight's assignment is slightly different than your others. Tonight, you will take your non-dominant hand and speak with your inner child in your journal. With your regular writing hand write this question at the top of the page, "What is it that you'd like to tell me?" Then, with your non-dominant hand, answer the question.

This is inner child work that you can do at any time. I have a journal full of dialogue with my inner child. Don't judge or think. Just write whatever comes to you. It's a process that truly works miracles. Give it a chance. I can tell you one thing, if you ever think about betraying yourself for someone else again, you will certainly think back to today's meditation. I hope that it helps you to love and protect yourself knowing that it's a small child that you are caring for. Know that you can do this kind of inner child work anytime in your journal.

Day 9: The Conscious Inventory

"Know who you are. Know what you want.
Know what you deserve. And don't settle for
less."
~Tony Gaskins

I'm sure you've set many goals in your life. You may have attained some or all of them! Yet, I'm wondering, have you ever sat down to ponder what you truly want, need, and desire, or have you simply settled for what's in front of you and tried to make that work?

Rescuers don't often think of themselves. They have an idea of what they want, need, or desire but they don't generally spend time thinking about this in depth because that would be way too much time on themselves. Here's the thing; if you don't ask yourself critical questions about what you want, need, and desire, how might you attract those experiences? The answer is, you won't. You will instead continue to focus on the needs, wants, and desires of others.

Now, I'm not saying that you have no goals in life. What I am saying is that today, you're going to spend some time thinking about what you really want, need, and desire. The only way to do this is to jump right in!

Conscious Inventory:

1. It is becoming easier for me to focus on my own needs, wants, and desires.

Strongly Disagree   *Disagree*   *Unsure*   *Agree*   *Strongly Agree*

2. I can see why it's important to set boundaries to serve myself that are clear and adhered to when crossed.

Strongly Disagree   *Disagree*   *Unsure*   *Agree*   *Strongly Agree*

3. I am open to looking at myself in a positive way to determine what is best for me.

Strongly Disagree   *Disagree*   *Unsure*   *Agree*   *Strongly Agree*

4. If I understood more of what I wanted, needed, and desired in this world, I wouldn't put myself in unhealthy relationships

Strongly Disagree   *Disagree*   *Unsure*   *Agree*   *Strongly Agree*

5. I understand that it's important for me to first love myself before pouring love out onto others.

Strongly Disagree   *Disagree*   *Unsure*   *Agree*   *Strongly Agree*

6. I am willing to look at myself in a non-critical way to heal my wounds.

Strongly Disagree   *Disagree*   *Unsure*   *Agree*   *Strongly Agree*

7. I believe that without clear boundaries that are upheld, I am only hurting myself.

Strongly Disagree   *Disagree*   *Unsure*   *Agree*   *Strongly Agree*

8. Completing mirror work daily is difficult at times but making a positive difference in my life.

Strongly Disagree   *Disagree*   *Unsure*   *Agree*   *Strongly Agree*

9. I understand that my inner child is the one person I must love and protect at all costs (aside from your own children).

Strongly Disagree   *Disagree*   *Unsure*   *Agree*   *Strongly Agree*

10. I am ready to take better care of myself.

Strongly Disagree   *Disagree*   *Unsure*   *Agree*   *Strongly Agree*

If you circled 5 or more *agree* or *strongly agree* responses, then you should give yourself a pat on the back or a great big hug because you are taking this 30-day commitment seriously and shifting your mind so that you will heal.

If you circled 5 or more *unsure* responses, stay the course. You are warming up to putting yourself first. Just trust the process and keep moving forward. Be sure to practice the ∞ tools daily.

If you circled 5 or more *disagree* or *strongly disagree* responses, then I must ask, who's been reading this book? Go back to Day 1 and really put the focus on you. You have the power within you to heal. However, you are the only one who can take the steps to do so.

Now that you are consciously aware of just how far you've come in eight short days, let's continue to shift your mindset and plant positive seeds!

Today's Exercise(s):

Today, you will complete a few exercises throughout your day. Exercise 1 can be done throughout the day because you will be adding to a list. Exercise 2 & 3 could be done either morning or evening. They may be done at the same time or at different times. It's up to you. Read ahead to see how you'd like to plan your day and then go for it!

Exercise 1: What do you truly like about yourself?

Take an honest inventory. Dig deep and make a list of 25 things that you like about yourself. It may seem difficult to make a list of 25, but think about this for a moment, when you love someone else, you can rattle off hundreds of things you like about them. Therefore, put the pen to the paper (or journal) and get going!

Here are some examples: I am funny. I am loving. I am kind. I have beautiful eyes. I am a good problem solver. I am sexy. I am a good mother. I am financially responsible. I am flexible. I am a good father. I am a good listener. I am an amazing cook (not me but maybe you). I am educated. I am passionate. I am compassionate. I am intuitive. I have beautiful hair. I am friendly. I am independent. I speak up for myself. I am intelligent. I have integrity. I am an animal and kid magnet. I am healthy. I am warm and welcoming.

Start with one and just allow yourself to flow with it. If you come up with more than 25, great! There's no penalty! Remember, it's not selfish, it's self-care. You must have at least 25, so keep working at this list until you attain at least 25. You've got this!

1. _____

_____

2. _____

_____

3. _____

_____

4. _____

_____

5. _____

_____

6. _____

_____

7. _____

_____

8. _____

_____

9. _____

_____

10. _____

_____

11. _____

_____

12. _____
_____

13. _____
_____

14. _____
_____

15. _____
_____

16. _____
_____

17. _____
_____

18. _____
_____

19. _____
_____

20. _____
_____

21. _____
_____

22. _____
_____

23. _____
_____

24. _____
_____

25. _____
_____

26. _____
_____

27. _____
_____

28. _____
_____

29. _____
_____

30. _____
_____

Exercise 2: Who I Am – Who I Want to Be

Now, you will answer the following questions as quickly as possible with the first thought that comes to mind.

Who are you? _____
_____
_____
_____

What are you? _____
_____

_____
_____

Where are you? _____

_____

_____

_____

Example:

Who are you? I am Vicki Savini

What are you? I am a mother, a teacher, a speaker, a coach, an author, a friend, a genuine, loving, caring woman.

Where am I? I am on the horizon of a new beginning.

And now, one more time...answer the following questions as soon as the thought pops into your mind. Don't overthink it, just let it flow. This is looking at your future self.

Who do you want to be? _____

_____

_____

_____

What do you want to be? _____

_____

_____

_____

Where do you want to be? _____

_____

_____

_____

Example:

Who do you want to be? My very best self in all aspects.

What do you want to be? A best-selling author ⍰.

Where do you want to be? Right where I am, on this journey of life.

*These exercises are just to get you revved up for the third exercise of the day, so please, do not overthink it. Just allow your thoughts to come to you without strain and write that down.

Exercise 3: The Big Kahuna!

In this exercise, you will need to sit and think in a quiet space. You can play soft music if you'd like but you really need quiet time to get to the core of your wants, needs, and desires. Focus on one area of your life; career, relationships, finances, etc. and go through the following questions. If you'd like to work on a few areas of your life, grab the PDF from the membership site and print as many as you'd like!

It's important to be very specific when you are filling out this paperwork because it is as if this is your letter to the Universe. (see example below)

My True Needs, Wants, & Desires

1) In this exercise you will first choose an area you'd like to focus on in your life to clearly define your needs, wants, and desires.

2) Next, you will list what you need. A need is essential to your happiness. Something you can't live without.

3) Then, list a few wants that relate to your topic of choice and the need that you're striving for. A want is a wish.

4) Finally, give your specific desire to the Universe (Remember Day 2? Focus on what you want instead of what you do not want and be very specific).

Example:

Topic you are focused on: Love Relationship

I need intimacy, availability, and security.

I want a man who only has eyes for me. A man who truly adores me and makes me the center of his world. Someone who is well balanced and emotionally available.

I desire to connect with a partner on every level; mind, body, and spirit. I will feel completely and totally loved by the man of my dreams. He is good looking on the inside and out. I feel at peace, safe, and totally loved and accepted by him. He lifts me up when I am down and holds my hand through life. He is always there for me and I am there for him. We lean on one another and support one another. We are best friends and exclusive lovers. Our love making is other worldly, as we are deeply connected in our hearts. We enjoy raising our family together and inspiring our children to be their best. We respect and love one another unconditionally. We are true partners in every sense of the word. We don't even need to communicate with words because our hearts and souls are united as one. We deeply appreciate one another, and we protect and love our relationship under all circumstances.

Together we rise and soar in every aspect of our lives. We make a great team and we are truly thankful for each other.

Whoa! Did you read the specs on that baby? Be specific. Ask and you shall receive! Your turn!

Needs, Wants, & Desires Worksheet

Topic you are focused on: _____

_____

(romantic relationships, family relationships, career, finances, health goals, etc.)

I need _____

_____

_____

_____

_____

_____

_____

_____

I want _____

_____

_____

_____

_____

_____

_____

_____

Be specific...What would that look like? If you're writing about your career, state the amount of money you'd like to make, the hours you want to work, etc. If relationship, give specific details. Ask for what you truly desire.

I desire _____

_____

_____

_____

_____

_____

_____

_____

_____

_____

_____

_____

_____

_____

Now, go have a great day with one thing in mind; focus on what you truly need, want, and desire. Don't ever settle for less.

You've got this!

Lots of Love & Tons of Light,

Vicki

Journal Entry: I am not assigning a specific journal entry today. If you feel the need to journal your thoughts and feelings, then have at it. Otherwise, I feel you've done enough writing for the day.

Day 10: You Can't Heal What You Don't Feel

"Always be true to your feelings because the more you deny what you are feeling, the stronger it becomes."
~Author Unknown

Feelings are real and important, yet from the time we were children we were taught to 'stuff' our feelings. I'm sure you remember this all too well. How many of you heard, "Stop crying or I'll give you something to cry about?" Perhaps it was, "Stop being a drama queen!" When someone is hurting, we want them to stop. No-one truly enjoys seeing others hurt (Well, some people do, but they are not right in the head, if you know what I mean). When it's your child and they are upset, you want to make it better as quickly as you can. However, at times you don't have the patience because you have your own stress, and this is where those above comments come from. Ultimately, hearing words of that nature teach us at a young age that we should hide our feelings. Men grew up hearing that boys shouldn't cry. Girls grew up being called drama queens or cry-babies if they allowed their emotions to show. This is an issue because our feelings are the barometer deep inside us that guide us to heal and the natural warning system that tells us when there's danger ahead.

When you push your feelings down because you are afraid to feel them in the moment you are only creating deeper issues. If you are familiar with Louise Hay's work, you know that when we ignore our feelings or bury them, we ultimately manifest dis-ease within our bodies. I write dis-ease because Louise taught us that the word disease means that the body is *out of ease.* Her work revealed that our negative thoughts create feelings that promote ill health within us. She went as far to say that cancer is long standing resentment held within the body, and I can personally attest to this. It has been scientifically proven that stress, anxiety and depression changes the cells in the body. It therefore doesn't seem impossible that we are inviting disease into our bodies by burying those feelings deep within because we are altering our cells. We are giving disease a comfortable home in our bodies. So, let's stop the nonsense and create an environment where disease is not welcome in our bodies!

Feel the Feeling

During your 30-day commitment, you have learned how to 'manage' feelings so you don't go down the rabbit hole or stay immobilized from feelings. You have learned the MIRROR process and the 80:20 rule which helps to turn negative thoughts around, so you won't get stuck in the muck. However, it's imperative to understand that you can't heal what you don't feel. By teaching you these tools, I'm not promoting the burial of feelings. Instead, I'm giving you tools to feel the feeling and then move through it, so you aren't immobilized by the darkest feelings. In today's exercise you will learn to feel, honor, and then release the feeling.

Let's talk about the dark feelings. The dark feelings are those that dim the inner light; sadness, anger, worry. These feelings are often triggered by an event that reminds us of that toxic core belief that dwells deep within. When we are triggered we begin to validate that core belief and it doesn't feel good. When we *react* to life it's as if we are having a knee jerk reaction. We are not processing what is happening. Instead, we are simply reacting to the event as quickly as it happens, and we lash out. When we *respond* to life, we take the time to process what's happening. This is what you have been learning with the MIRROR process, the 80:20 rule, and other tools. You have been learning to take life as it comes and respond instead of reacting. When we are reacting to life, it's important to note, that this is not the adult responding to the experience. Instead, this is your inner child calling out for help because they are hurting. It is as if you are kicking and screaming on the inside. Every time you feel triggered, you now know that this is your little kid within and you have todays tool and many more to re-parent that child.

When the dark feelings come up for you, don't push them down or try to ignore them. If you do this, those feelings will only deepen and bubble up to the surface coming back with a vengeance. Feel the feeling with every fiber of your being and use the exercise below to help you honor the feeling and release it.

Today's Exercise:

This exercise should be completed in the morning, if at all possible, so you can reflect throughout the day and journal in the evening.

1) Think about an experience or event that triggers you and tempts you to go down the rabbit hole. Maybe it's a person, a situation, or a thought.

2) *Example: Feeling ignored triggers me to believe that I'm not important.*

3) Complete this meditation (record your voice, have someone read it to you, or click on Day 10 on the membership site).

Today's Meditation

Close your eyes and take a deep breath in through your nose and release it through your mouth. Breathe in again and release slowly. Feel the feeling of the event that triggers you. Allow this feeling to well up in your body, truly feeling it in every fiber of your being. Keep breathing through it – in through your nose and out through your mouth. Get a clear picture in your mind of this situation, experience, or event so that you may feel every aspect of the dark feelings that come with it. Continue to breathe in and release out. Where do you feel this welling up in your body the most? Is it in your head, your throat, your heart, your stomach? Imagine a ball of energy in that spot where these dark feelings are settling. What does this feeling have to do with your core toxic belief? How does it relate to this belief? How is it validating this toxic seed even further? Breathe in and release out. Imagine that ball of energy again. Give it a color. See the color in your mind's eye and breathe pure, clean energy into this ball of energy. As you breathe in, imagine the white light from previous meditations coming to this area and consuming the ball of dark energy. Breathe in deeply and release. As you breathe in, take in the white light and remember that you are whole, perfect, and complete, just as you are. As you breathe out, release the negative energy, reminding yourself the opposite of your toxic seed. I am important, I am safe, I am worthy, I am enough, I am lovable. Breathe in again, fill your whole body with white light. Breathe out and release. Repeat this breathing pattern three more times. In through the nose, out through the mouth. In through the nose, out through the mouth. One more time, in through the nose, out through the mouth. Imagine yourself holding the child within one more time. Whisper in their ear the message that comes to you. Remind them that you are there for them and that you've got this. Tell them they are safe, loved, important, worthy, and enough – more than enough – they are perfect just the way they are. Breathe in and release out. Breathe in, and out. Breathe again. Open your eyes.

1) Throughout your day, if a dark feeling comes up for you again, ask yourself what it has to do with your toxic core belief and simply think of holding your inner child and whispering to them what you truly need to hear.

Now, go have a great day with one thing in mind; feel your feelings because you can't heal what you don't feel!

You've got this!

Lots of Love & Tons of Light,

Vicki

Journal Entry: Tonight, journal about your experiences throughout the day. Share how you will use this tool in the future to remind yourself to *respond* to life instead of reacting to it.

Day 11: Tap it Out

*"You can grow if you're willing to feel
awkward and uncomfortable when you try
something new."*

~Brian Tracy

Yesterday, I asked you to feel the feelings. I know it may not have been very comfortable for you but I'm proud of you for getting through it. There are times when the feelings can overwhelm you. You may have experienced a crisis or are facing a very difficult situation. It's not easy to reset the mind when you're overwhelmed and in full-on fear mode. When this occurs, I reach for the next tool that you will add to your toolbox. This tool is called, tapping. Now, I'm not expecting you to put on a pair of tap shoes and start tapping your way across the floor. That would be fun, but that's not the kind of tapping I'm referring to. I am referring to EFT (Emotional Freedom Technique). Emotional

Freedom Technique is one of the most popular forms of energy psychology that was developed in the 90's by Gary Craig. He is a Stanford engineering graduate specializing in healing and self-improvement. This process involves tapping specific meridian points on your body with your fingertips while thinking of a problem or issue and voicing positive affirmations. It has been scientifically proven to clear emotional blocks from your body's bioenergy system to restore mind and body balance. Clinical studies reveal that EFT is able to rapidly reduce the emotional impact of memories and incidence of emotional distress. In this chapter, I'm going to give you the basics to get started. I'm not a person who needs the science behind tools because I generally go by what *feels* right in my experiences, and when I tried EFT it worked like a charm. However, I do understand that some prefer the scientific background, so I'm sending you to the experts. If you are interested in learning more about tapping (a.k.a. EFT-Emotional Freedom Technique), please visit www.thetappingsolution.com or simply google or YouTube the topic. There's tons of great information out there on this specific tool if you'd like to research further or watch a few videos. If you're like me and you just want to experience the relief immediately, then continue reading.

The Basics

EFT dissolves the energy associated with the painful feelings while healing the physical body by 'tapping' your nervous system.

1) You begin by considering what your most pressing issue (MPI) is. This is the situation, thought or concern that is causing you emotional discord.

2) On a scale of 0-10, how much do you feel this pain in your body (yes, emotional pain is considered pain as well)

3) Create a set up statement: *Even though* _____, *I still deeply and completely love and approve of myself.*

4) Then you go through the tapping points and talk yourself through the problem (don't worry, I'm going to give you a specific example to follow).

5) When you're finished with one cycle, you ask yourself how much pain you now feel in your body regarding this issue 0-10 (it should be less).

6) If you need another round, go for it until the fear and anxiety dissolve or at least lessen.

For our purposes you are going to work on dissolving your core toxic belief. However, if you go to the above website you can find other examples on general beliefs, thoughts, and feelings. If you are signed up for the membership, I have also included a video where I show you my tapping process.

On the following page I have created a diagram for you. Use this diagram (or one from the resources online) to begin your tapping process. Let's start tapping!

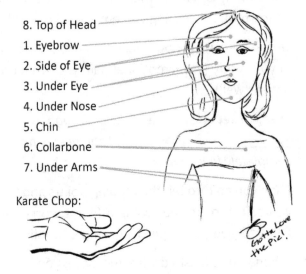

8. Top of Head
1. Eyebrow
2. Side of Eye
3. Under Eye
4. Under Nose
5. Chin
6. Collarbone
7. Under Arms

Karate Chop:

Gotta Love the Pic!

Today's Exercise:

Your first endeavor today with tapping is to deal with this core toxic seed that's been causing so much havoc in your life over the years. I will walk you through this process step by step.

1) Your MPI (Most Pressing Issue) is your core toxic belief: I'm not important, I'm not safe, I'm not worthy, I'm not enough, or I'm not lovable. When you think of your MPI, I want you to think of a time when it caused issues for you and allow yourself to feel the darkness of those feelings. Allow the anxiety and pain to rise in your body and then begin.

2) Look at the diagram to see where the 'karate chop' point is and begin to tap those points on both hands as if you are gently banging them together and repeat this phrase; *"Even though I've had this toxic belief that I am not _____ for years, I still deeply and completely love and approve of myself."* Now, repeat two more times.

3) Now, take your index finger and middle finger (tall man) and gently tap between your eyebrows and say, *"This belief that I am not _____ has caused a lot of havoc in my life."*

4) Next, continue using the same finger but use both hands (one on either side of your eyes and move to position 2. Say, *"I've had enough of this*

belief. It's time to shift this belief and start making positive changes for me."

5) Move to position 3, under the eyes, using both hands. Say the opposite of your toxic belief (ex. *I'm not important turns into I AM Important*). Repeat two more times.

6) Move to position 4, using one hand. Say, *"I know I am* _____ *because* _____." Give yourself positive praise from this point forward.

7) Move to position 5, the chin and continue to praise yourself.

8) Move to position 6, closing your hands like fists (like a gorilla gently pounding on its chest) and say, *"I am stronger than I believed. I can heal. I am healing and changing for the better every day."*

9) Move to position 7, crossing your arms across your heart and tapping under each of your arm pits. Say, *"I've got this. I am becoming my own hero. I have the tools to be my best self. I am* _____." (insert the opposite of your toxic belief).

10) Move to position 8, top of the head, using one hand. Say, *"I am* _____." (the opposite of your core toxic belief).

11) Take a deep breath in and ask yourself how your pain/anxiety is within your body at this point. It should've decreased. If you still feel anxious, then start the process again and repeat until you have calmed down.

Whew, that was an exercise to decrease the anxiety around this core toxic seed that we are working to rip out of your garden of life. If you would like to see other examples of how to use EFT to calm yourself when your feelings are overwhelming, you go to www.thetappingsolution.com or click on day 11 on the membership site.

Now, go have a great day with one thing in mind; when you're triggered, you can tap it out.

You've got this!

Lots of Love & Tons of Light,

Vicki

Journal Entry: Write a list of other MPI's that you could tap out. Perhaps try more tapping this evening and journal your thoughts and feelings from tapping.

*This is a tool you may want to add to your daily practice. I did not include this only because I feel that it needs to be a choice.

If you are a member, go to the site and click on Day 11 for my personal tapping video.

Day 12: MYOB (Mind Your Own Business), Really

"There are some things in this universe best left alone."
~Joseph Derepentigny

You already know it's difficult to focus on yourself. You've come to terms with that and you are now working hard to keep the focus on you. Likely, you have heard the saying, 'Mind your own business.' Yes? As rescuers, we tend to stick our noses where they really don't belong. Of course, we're not being nosy. We are simply trying to help or make things better in some way. Eh eh. Not a good idea. There are three distinct ways rescuers sabotage themselves by over-stepping their bounds; 1) We are always ready to help, even when others aren't looking for help, 2) We concern ourselves with what others think about us, and 3) We don't let go easily when it's time to let go.

Here I Am to Save the Day

I get it. You've worn this cape for a very long time. You snap it on without even realizing it anymore, but perhaps it's time to step back. As rescuers, we want to help everyone in front of us. We are good-natured, loving, and compassionate. In our minds, we honestly believe that we are trying to be helpful, but there are many times when we should just sit back, zip the lips, and not offer solutions. We are so accustomed to snapping on the cape that the moment someone appears to have a problem, our minds go into solution mode. We listen to part of the conversation then immediately come up with a plan of action. Sometimes, people are putting their problems out there because they are venting and just need to get it out. Others are baiting us because they have come to learn that if they put the bait out, we'll nab it, and solve the problem for them! Either way, *their* problem is not *our* problem. Yet, we sometimes make it our own whether they ask for help or not. It's common for a rescuer to feel overwhelmed. They take on way too much because they believe they must solve the problems of the world. Truth be told, you don't need to solve those problems. You need to stay in your own lane and focus on you and yours if you want to be happy, healthy, and balanced. As difficult as it is, today you are going to bite your tongue. When people are sharing their story, just breathe in, close your lips tightly, and then breathe out slowly. Allow them to simply share their story and don't offer a solution unless the other person specifically asks for your help. Then, and only then, is it acceptable for you to offer a solution. Otherwise, let people solve their own damn problems unless the problem directly relates to you. *Even* if the problem relates to you, be careful not to guide them and offer the solution if you have set a boundary and they are dangerously close to crossing it. Remember that you set clear boundaries to serve yourself and be sure *your* needs are met. Don't solve problems for anyone else.

What Did I Do?

Rescuers are also uber-sensitive. We think we must be privy to what everyone else thinks of us. We want to know why people ignore us, treat us poorly, or have a negative opinion of us. The moment a person starts to distance themselves or not include us, we begin to wonder what it is that we've done to change the climate of the relationship. We are always looking to blame ourselves in some way and so we begin to imagine that we have done something wrong. If I only did this or that, then maybe the relationship wouldn't have changed. Rescuers are damn hard on themselves. The truth of the matter is, it's not always about you. That's right. I know it's hard to believe but everyone's got their own shit going on and if they really have a problem with you, they'll eventually tell you. If they don't, then they weren't worth your time anyways. Part of loving yourself is being able to look in the mirror and like the person staring back at you no matter what. Some people are going to love you. Some are going to be triggered by you and some are just not going to like you. It doesn't really matter. What matters most is how you see yourself and your opinion of you should not be determined by what others think or say. Take what others think or say into consideration, but don't allow it to be your absolute truth. For years, you've believed that your value and worth was determined by how much you could do for others. How'd that work out for you? Today, if someone seems distant or is snubbing you in some way, just take a deep breath, walk away, and repeat your affirmations for the day. Your happiness is not determined by what others think, feel, or value about you. Give them the space to feel what they are feeling and just focus on you.

If It's Toxic, Step Away

Finally, rescuers believe that they must know as much as possible about any situation to move through it or away from it. Sometimes, we even dig for information long after a relationship or situation is over because we are still trying to comprehend what happened or prove to ourselves that we didn't do anything wrong. We spend our precious time concerned over what others are doing instead of what we need to do. We may get a sense or a feeling in our gut that something is not right and instead of just believing that and moving away from this person or situation, we begin to dig deep in search of the truth. Unfortunately, that often leads to more issues as we may uncover truth that we really didn't need to know because it only hurts us even more. Trust yourself. When something doesn't feel right, it isn't right. You don't need proof beyond the actions that you are seeing. When a situation unfolds, and you've gotten the raw end of the deal, count your losses and your blessings then, move on. When a relationship ends that's toxic keep your eyes ahead of you and don't look back. That basically means, don't look at your ex's social media or try to find out what's going on with them. You will only end up hurt in the long run because you will question – once again – what you could've done differently. It's the whole anchor scenario from the beginning of the book. When that anchor is soaring through the air getting ready to plunge into the sea, don't hold on. Let that shit go. When something is done; a situation, a business deal, or a relationship, let it be done. Sometimes, it's best to keep moving forward without looking back.

Today's Exercise:

You learned three distinct ways that rescuers sabotage themselves by not minding their own business; they offer solutions when it isn't warranted, they care too much about what others think, and they have a hard time letting go and stepping away until they get to what they feel is the absolute truth (and even then, they don't always let shit go). Today, you will stay in your own lane and keep the focus on you;

1) When someone is sharing a story, take a breath, bite down and don't offer a solution unless the other person specifically asks for your input. Remember that you do not have to solve the problems of the world. No need to add more to your plate and take on a side dish of overwhelm. Stepping back isn't selfish. It's self-care.

2) Keep in mind that it's really none of your business what others think about you. What matters most is how you see yourself and what others think, feel, or value about you does *not* determine your worth.

3) When it's done, let it go. Eyes forward and no looking back. You've done all that you could do – honestly – just keep putting one foot in front of the other and don't look over your shoulder. The past is the past. The future isn't here yet. Today is all you truly have. Stay in the moment

and remember to always ask yourself that critical question; is this serving me or sabotaging me?

Reminder: Be sure you are using your ∞ tools daily. You must fill your tank if you want to shift your perspective and love yourself. It's the only way to burn this damn cape!

Now, go have a great day with one thing in mind; MYOB (Mind Your Own Business). It's really the best way for you to focus on yourself.

You've got this!

Lots of Love & Tons of Light,

Vicki

Journal Entry: What was most challenging for you today while trying to mind your own business and stay in your own lane?

Day 13: Too Many Balls in the Air

"If it doesn't add to your life, it doesn't belong in your life." G. Batiste

I don't know about you but in my life; I've taken on way too much, had high expectations of myself, and wanted immediate results to check things off my list. It's no wonder that I felt so overwhelmed at times. I've been hard on myself because I wanted to do everything right and never wanted to let anyone down. That was the rescuer in me. Funny, in that equation where the hell was I taking care of me? By allowing myself to get overwhelmed so frequently, I wasn't loving myself. Instead, I was taking on more than my share, putting too much pressure on myself, and validating my toxic core belief. That's no way to treat a hero! It's time to add another tool to your toolbox of life to rid you of the "O" word.

You likely juggle several balls in the air daily. You almost always have a lot going on. Life is like a buffet to you. You see it laid out, and you want it all. You add too much to your plate and it begins to feel unbearably heavy. Rescuers not only want it all, but they want to be everything to everyone. As stated in the last chapter, you are likely to feel overwhelmed in your life. You know you've felt it. It's become part of a cycle for you. You say you're going to simplify your life. You take a few steps to do so, then you say yes too many times and boom, you're right back to the "O" word again. You know what I'm talking about; that feeling like someone is sitting on your chest, your heart begins to race, and your head is spinning. You are *overwhelmed*. Rescuers feel this feeling all too often because they give too much and run themselves ragged.

There are a few reasons you juggle all these balls and get overwhelmed; you have a hard time saying no, you want immediate results, and you believe your worth is based on what you can do to serve others. By now, you likely know why you do this to yourself, right? You are a people pleaser. You want everyone to like you and you want to be the 'go to guy or gal'. You've been in this role for a long time and you've set yourself up to believe that your worth is dependent upon caring for others and keeping all your balls in the air. Many of those balls that are in the air are only in your lineup because you are running from your toxic core belief. The blessing is that you now have the power because you are aware of that pesky little seed. You are no longer in the darkness. The light has been shone upon your garden of life and you can now weed and re-seed.

Perhaps it's time to let a few of those balls drop and only juggle the ones that validate your *new* positive beliefs about yourself.

Just Say No

You may feel like everyone wants something from you and not many are available to reciprocate, but why is that? Where did this come from? I hate to break it to you, but it came from you. You hardly ever say no! You absolutely know when you are taking on too much, but you cannot bring yourself to say no because you are a problem solver – you know you can get it done and you don't want to let anyone down. Repeat after me, "The answer is no." Even when you have tried to say no to people in the past, you have repeatedly apologized and then backed yourself into a corner only to end up saying yes out of pure guilt. Say it with me again, "No!" You don't need to explain yourself or apologize. You simply say, "No." You can be gentle and say, "I'd really like to help you with this, but I have to say no at this time." Nuff said. No need to explain anymore. You know that you already have too much on your plate and if this isn't something that is serving you, then you need to nix it and move on. Remember, you are not here to solve the problems of the world. You can be a light to the world, help to heal others, be a teacher, mentor, or friend but – you do not need to solve everyone's problems. That's what has put you in this rescuer position in the first place. The first exercise you will focus on today is saying no to things that do not serve you. This is the beginning to prioritizing. The only way to drop some of those balls in the air is to learn to prioritize.

Right Here, Right Now

Being a problem solver is a beautiful thing. It gives you the opportunity to come up with fast, efficient ideas on a moment's notice. You always have good ideas. You may not necessarily know how to execute them to completion at that moment, but you will certainly figure it out. You are hard on yourself. You want everything to happen right here, right now. Patience is a virtue, but it might not be something that you've mastered just yet. Once you get a great idea, you light up and you're ready to go. Come on, hurry up, let's get this party started. You are a mover and a shaker. Nothing can stop you once you get rolling. Problem is, you want everything to be okay immediately and you get impatient when things aren't going the way you thought they would. Couple that with not wanting to let anyone down and boy do you have a disaster! This goes back to putting too much on your plate, but you've already committed and won't back down. Patience. Your second lesson for today revolves around patience. The middle of prioritizing.

Am I Worth It?

You have spent your whole life feeling that your worth is dependent on how others see you, feel about you, and what they say about you. You have been taught that your value goes up when you please others and serve them in some way. Eh, it's nice to be kind, loving and warm, but let's do that from our hearts and not from a place of lack. If you have put your worth in the hands of others, you have been sabotaging yourself. You see, you may not realize this, but you teach people how to treat you. If you allow them to walk all over your boundaries, you have taught them to disrespect you. If you are constantly available and you break other commitments to be there for your object of affection, then you are teaching them that you are at their beck and call. When you are not loving yourself, others learn not to love you. Put yourself first, do what serves you, and give only from your heart – not seeking approval – and you will see a major shift in your life. You are worth it. Yet, the only way to feel that is to put yourself first before you begin to reach out to help others. And, never, no never, betray yourself for the sake of another again.

First Thing's First

I can't tell you how many times I've gotten overwhelmed in a week! I'm a single mom, a first-grade teacher, a mom of two dogs, a home owner, a life coach, a mentor, a friend, a sister, a daughter, oh yes, and an author too! I could add to that list for days, as I'm sure you could as well. It's easy to feel overwhelmed because we wear so many hats in a day. So how is it that we are supposed to drop some of these balls in the air? Prioritize!

The house needs to be cleaned, the bills are stacking up, new flyers need to go out for the business, your kid needs new sneakers, baseball practice is at 5, someone needs to make dinner, and the dogs need to be fed. Yep! It's all true. It's all reality. However, what needs to be done in this very moment? As I stated above, I wear a lot of hats. The only way for me to stay sane (and that's still up for debate) is to prioritize my to-do list and stay in the moment. Today, you're going to learn about my priority sandwich. This will teach you how to prioritize so you don't get overwhelmed.

All the tools you've learned so far and all the tools to come are giving you more options. You are in the drivers' seat. You no longer need to choose others first. You don't need their approval to be your best self. All you need is your own approval.

Today's Exercise:

Today you will focus on setting your priorities straight. I know you wear several hats. Wear them well and only one at a time. Be in the moment with each hat that you put on and don't add extras that don't belong in your pile. You've got enough to juggle.

1) Write out the following in your journal, on a blank sheet of paper or grab the PDF from the membership site www.vickisavini.com/member.

a) Write the date in the middle of the cloud.

b) On each line (arm) add something that is on your mind that's weighing you down. This could be things that need to be done, issues that need to be handled, relationships that need perspective, etc. If you need to add more lines (arms), have at it.

c) After filling in the arms, walk away for a few minutes and get your day started.

d) Go back to the paper and circle the one arm (line) that needs your immediate attention. What is the one area on that sheet that you need to focus on first.

e) Then write numbers next to the others in order of importance. If there is anything on a line (arm) that isn't adding you your life in a positive way, delete it. Simply scratch it off your list.

2) Keep your paper with you throughout the day. Stay the course and allow your focus to go to the number one area you chose in the morning. Today's focus will be on serving yourself a delicious *Priority Sandwich*. Allow me to teach you how to whip one of those bad boys up!

3) ***The top bun:*** If you are tempted to add something to your plate, step back and ask yourself if you are serving yourself or sabotaging yourself by doing so. If you are serving yourself and it will lighten your load, then go for it. If you are sabotaging and it will add to the load, say, "No," and do not apologize or explain.

4) ***The middle (juiciest part of the sandwich):*** Be patient. When ideas come up or when you are striving to get something done and it's not

going fast enough. Take a deep breath, then say your affirmations. Keep in mind that what is for you, will not pass you by and know that it is all happening for your highest good, in Divine timing. Ask yourself if this event needs to happen right now or if it can wait. A huge part of prioritization is sticking to your most pressing issue and putting everything else in line behind that to be handled.

5) ***The bottom bun:*** Remember that your worth is not determined by what you can do for others, how they see you, or what they have to say about you. Throughout the day, consistently say your new core belief (ex. I am important, I am safe, I am lovable, I am enough, or I am worthy). Allow that to be the download that you have on repeat. This will certainly take your worth out of the hands of others and give you back your power. Be sure you are constantly and consistently asking yourself if your thoughts and actions are serving you or sabotaging you. If you remember nothing else from this book, please remember this one sentence, "*Is this serving me or sabotaging me?*"

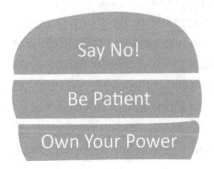

Say No!

Be Patient

Own Your Power

6) At the end of the day, look at your priority sheet again and see how you did. If you are still on the verge of overwhelm, then continue with this exercise tomorrow and the day after, and after, until you can eat that *Priority Sandwich* like a champ!

Now, go have a great day with one thing in mind; prioritize! Say no, be patient, and own your power.

You've got this!

Lots of Love & Tons of Light,

Vicki

Journal Entry: How am I feeling about the "O" word? Was I overwhelmed at all today? How did I handle that? How can I incorporate the *Priority Sandwich* into my day to prevent overwhelm?

Side Note: Want to hear something funny? While writing this chapter (Day 13) it was ironically Friday, the 13th. It had been a bit of an interesting day. We were working on the design of the book cover and the graphic designer wasn't quite getting the message I was trying to convey. In the past, this would've really ruined my day and took me down the rabbit hole because of my impatience and fear of not accomplishing my task. However, this time, I took a deep breath and said, "It's all going to work out for the highest good." I decided to reach out to my publisher to show him the design and get his thoughts. Within minutes he came up with a few designs of his own that were quite amazing because he *knew* what I was conveying in the book (hence the gorgeous cover design). In the meantime, I was teaching my first graders at school – juggling, if you will. I had to prioritize and be in the moment. It was the only way to rise. Later that evening, I had my mom hat on; had to get dinner together in between writing, walk and feed the dogs and then bathe the dogs (that was an adventure). The whole time I was thinking, 'I've got to write tonight.' Instead of getting frazzled and overwhelmed, as I had in the past, I stayed in the moment and prioritized. After bathing the dogs, I tried to sit to write once more and now I had writers block. Really Universe? Again, this would have shaken me in the past, but now I've got my toolbox! I stepped away from the computer and went to take a nice, long, hot aromatherapy shower (boy do I love those).

While in the shower, enjoying the smell of peppermint, the words for this chapter just came crashing in. The beauty of this book is that I know it works because I lived it and I'm honored to share the tools with you. I learned to love myself and be my own hero and that's why I am confident that you can too. Prioritize. Listen to yourself and honor what you need. And this, my friends, leads us right up to Day 14!

Day 14: Pamper Yourself Because You Matter

"You can't always expect others to treat you right, but you can treat yourself right."
~Bryant McGill

Now that you're figuring out that priorities are important to prevent you from feeling overwhelmed and leading you down the rabbit hole, let's get one thing straight; you need to be your number one priority. Ouch! I know that might still sting, even though you've been through 13 days on this journey, but you *must* be at the top of the list. Remember when we talked about filling your tank? If you are not filling your own tank, then it is like your car breaking down on the side of the road. We've run on empty for years, never truly taking the time to fill ourselves to keep the vehicle running. We've broken down on the side of the road countless times only to realize that we are the ones who need to pick ourselves back up. Think back to my airplane story. Remember the story when my son was four months old? If you're not putting the oxygen mask on yourself, then how on earth will you be able to help others? When you are not taking the time to honor your own needs, you are speeding through life haphazardly, traveling way too fast and missing the beauty right in front of you. Time out! It's time for you to pamper yourself. I know that you want to be your best self. You are a caring, loving person, and you want to be able to help others without defeating yourself. The only way to do this is to fill your own damn tank first. Today, you will pamper yourself.

What does that look like for you? When I am feeling like I'm running on empty, I know that it's time for me to take a time out. That might mean a day to myself away from everyone or a few hours sitting in a bookstore. Whatever relaxes you and brings you back to center is what you need to do for yourself today. Hopefully, this lesson will help you to be proactive and see that by planning time ahead for yourself and giving your mind, body, and soul what is needed, you won't have to worry about that "O" word!

Right Back at 'Cha

You certainly know how to pamper others. You listen to their needs, plan to make sure that they are well taken care of and try to make their lives easier and less stressful. You take the time to give them what you believe they need, want, and desire. Now, it's your turn.

Your mind. What is it that puts your mind at ease or stimulates it in a healthy way? For me, I know that if I am not writing and reading, I feel out of balance. I take time every day to write by either writing; a blog, a workshop, a journal entry or, even a book! Writing is cathartic for me. It helps me to process what is happening in my life and allows me to take a step back from worry and stress. I have also learned that reading helps me to calm down, as well as stimulate my mind by stretching it and inspiring me. What is it for you that either eases or stimulates your mind in a healthy way?

Your body. It's important to listen to your body. So many people ignore the warning signs of stress and disease because they are not taking time for themselves. Stop, breathe, and listen to your body. What is it that your body needs to feel alive and healthy? Is it a certain kind of food? Perhaps, some type of movement? I myself, have never loved to exercise. It's just not a thing that I look forward to. However, I do realize that a body in motion stays in motion, and so I make sure that I am active. I also listen to my body clearly without question. If I feel tired, I rest. If I feel anxious, I do a calming activity; I go to yoga, take a hot aromatherapy shower, or I meditate. Listen to what your body needs in that moment and don't hesitate to do what feels right. What is it for you that calms or energizes your body, dependent on your goal?

Your Spirit. What is it that your soul is calling for? This is about listening to yourself and trusting that you know what's right for you. You don't question this when it comes to helping others, so why do you question it for yourself? Find a way to tap into your higher self. For some, that might be attending a church service, while others, it may be a walk outside communing with nature. It doesn't matter what you do to connect if you understand that we are all connected to something bigger. When I feel 'disconnected' from Spirit, I reach for something uplifting to read, I meditate, grab a pendulum or angel cards, and quiet my mind so my soul can be heard. I do whatever feels right; paint, write, read, sleep, walk, relax, etc. What is it that your soul needs to feel peaceful?

Today's Exercise:

Your mission today is to pamper your mind, body, and Spirit.

1) *Choose one way to relax or inspire your mind and go for it.*

Inspire your mind by; reading, writing, attending a workshop, engaging in interesting conversation, listen to a TedTalk, read poetry, learn something new, attend a class, teach a class, go to a bookstore and read random books, or perhaps just sit in nature and be in the moment.

2) *Do something kind and loving for your body.*

Spend extra time doing mirror work naked, attend an exercise class, go to yoga, get a massage, lay in the sun, sleep, relax outdoors, go for a run, eat a healthy meal from an expensive restaurant, eat ice cream for dinner or have really great sex!

3) *Connect yourself with Spirit.*

Listen to what your soul wants and needs and simply be willing. Attend a seminar or a church service, commune with nature, play the guitar, listen to music, walk in nature, meditate, pray, balance yourself with crystals, pull some angel cards, or listen to something uplifting and positive.

Today is your day to simply listen to your inner wisdom and reward yourself for being you!

Now, go have a great day with one thing in mind; pamper yourself. Taking care of you isn't selfish, it's self-care (a.k.a. self-love).

You've got this!

Lots of Love & Tons of Light,

Vicki

Journal Entry: What did I notice by pampering myself? How often do I need to do this? What have I learned from today?

Day 15: Jump, Laugh, Play

*"The kid in you holds the key to living a rich
and full life. Let him or her out to play"*
~Cheryl Richardson

When was the last time you laughed? I don't mean a half smile or a smirk. I'm talking about a belly laugh where you think you might've peed your pants. We don't smile, laugh, or feel enough joy, and that's because we've all forgotten how to play. My dad always used to say, "Smile and the world smiles with you." He also said, with a twinkle in his eyes, "Smile because you'll make people wonder what you're up to!" But that's a whole different story. We need to smile, people. We need to feel joy and the sweet release of laughter. Without playing we become stagnant. Who ever said you needed to stop playing and enjoying life once you became an adult? That's a tragedy. Don't listen!

The greatest compliment I ever received was that I see the world through the eyes of a child. I was given this compliment because I have always been able to understand what children are feeling, see the child within everyone, and stay in touch with the child within myself. One of my fondest memories was trying to shop on Black Friday at Toys R Us with my sister and niece. We had never attempted this before and we somehow thought going to a toy store on this blessed day would be a good idea. We walked into the store (after waiting in a long line for 40 minutes) only to find people fighting over carts and bumping into one another. Not my kind of shopping experience. My sister and niece only went along for this excursion to help *me* shop for my son. As we saw the chaos, we looked at each other and giggled. We then tried to navigate the store and fill our cart. It appeared everything on my list wasn't on sale, and if it was on sale, it was already gone. People were in awful moods and extremely rude. It was almost as bad as waiting in line at Disney for a ride on a hot day! We only had two items in the cart after 45 minutes when we noticed that the checkout line was literally wrapped around the store. That's when I spied a red Radio Flyer wagon in the middle of an aisle. My eyes lit up and I pushed the cart aside. I glanced at my 19-year old niece and said, "Hop in!" My niece eagerly hopped in the wagon as my sister shook her head and began to laugh. She knows me all too well and had a clear idea of what was coming next. I grabbed the handle and we were off; running through the store, weaving in and out of people, laughing like a couple of school kids. We did that until an employee strongly advised us to park the wagon. We smiled and nodded, then headed to Applebee's for some appetizers and drinks. It was clear that the situation was way too serious for us, so we made light of it and acted like little kids. Boy, that was a great memory. When I think back to that evening I always smile because instead of allowing the frustration of the situation to get to me, I unleashed the little kid within. This gave me the opportunity to turn a tortuous memory into a fond memory.

We all have this tool deep inside of us. We can always let the little kid out, but we refrain due to fear of what others will think or say. Part of getting naked and comfortable in your own skin is letting your inner child play. How can you let the kid out today? What did you love to do as a child? Today, you will go back to that feeling of freedom and pure joy. If you didn't have this experience in your childhood, then today is your day to re-create a childhood memory. After all, it's never too late to create a happy childhood. Hopefully, once you unleash the kid within, you'll want to do that more and more.

How to Unleash the Kid Within

Most kids are unaware that adults are even in their presence. They see something that looks interesting and they just go to that without hesitation. They are curious about the world around them and they are constantly looking for opportunities to play. Life is fun. They want to know how things work and what makes the world go around. They want to jump, laugh, and play. Adults can do that too. We get into the real world and suddenly everything gets so serious. We have mounting pressure on us and crushing responsibility and so we begin to forget what fun and laughter is. That's when the "O" word seeps into our world and from there, I don't have to tell you what comes next. Maybe if we lightened up a bit, we would be able to handle the pressure and responsibility better. Your attitude about life can make or break you. Today, let's get in touch with the kid within. I'm going to share some of the things I do to let the little kid out daily. Use these ideas or come up with your own. No matter what, you're getting out of your comfort zone and learning to love yourself on a whole other level.

You've got to do the grocery shopping and you're in a time crunch. Music makes the world go 'round. Why don't you sing through the aisles? Go ahead. It doesn't matter if the Voice is calling you or if dogs begin to howl when you sing your tune, just let it out. If they escort you out of the store, just smile and laugh and check that off to an experience you'll never forget!

Not into singing? Ok, plug your earbuds in and create a fun playlist. Dance your way through the store. Who cares who's looking. Just focus on the music and your list. Who knows, you might even brighten someone else's day.

You're walking out of the parking lot and it starts to rain. You're going to have to step it up a bit. Hop on the cart, peddle with one foot, then ride the cart with glee through the lot. Woo hoo! You're a kid again.

You're walking through a shopping center and feeling a little bored. You see an escalator with the stairs coming downward. You're already downstairs but you want to go up. Challenge yourself. Start running UP the down escalator until you get to the top! (I actually did this in 4" heels – it was exhilarating when I finally reached the top)

You've had a rough day and it's time to pick up the kids from daycare. You arrive and the kids are still engaged in play. Stop for a moment and just watch them. Then, go sit (or lay) in the middle of the floor. Just let the kids play around you, on you, or join in to their fun. This will lift your spirits every time.

It's a hot day and you forgot to bring your lunch. Not much time to stand in line but you see a froyo (frozen yogurt) shop. Grab some froyo for lunch and be sure to add all the goodies and lots of whipped cream!

Smell a box of crayons, color a mandala, skip down the street, join your kids in a game they are playing, do a few cartwheels (don't hurt yourself), start a water balloon war, draw with chalk on the sidewalk, or run through a sprinkler on a hot day. It doesn't matter what you do, as long as you let that little kid come out to play!

Today's Exercise:

Read, record your voice, then listen, or go to the membership site (www.vickisavini.com/member) to complete the following meditation.

Sit or lay down in a quiet space. Take a deep breath in through your nose and release it out through your mouth. Breathe in again and imagine your breath entering your body and landing in your lungs. Fill your lungs like a balloon and then release the air slowly from your mouth. Breathe in again and release. Imagine there is a white light flowing over the top of your head. Feel the warmth of this light like sunshine on a warm summer's day. Breathe in through your nose and release slowly through your mouth. Imagine that light flowing down over your face, around your neck and down your shoulders. Feel this light like a gentle massage rolling over your shoulders, relaxing your body completely. Breathe in and allow the light to fill your entire body. Breathe out and feel the release. Breathe in again and then release and relax. Imagine a bubble around you. Feel the lightness of this bubble. Envision yourself gently lifting and floating through the air – back in time – to your childhood. See the trees beneath you and the sky around you. Feel the wind in your hair and the sun on your face. Think back to the time when you were growing and learning. A time when life was simple, and laughter came easier. Go to the first memory that comes to you when you were laughing and enjoying life as a child. Feel the joy and lightness of the moment. If you are struggling to get to your own happy memory, then go to the first memory you have of a child that is belly laughing. It could be a relative, a neighborhood child, a student, a friend's child or perhaps your own. Just allow yourself to become immersed in the laughter. Feel the lightness of the moment and the excitement in their giggle. Take a deep breath in and release it out. Breathe in again, feeling this happy and joyful energy pass throughout your entire body. Keep breathing in through your nose and out through your mouth and when you are ready, open your eyes.

What is it that you can do today that will make you feel like a kid again? Is it eating ice cream for lunch or dinner? Could it be finger painting or drawing on the sidewalk with chalk? Maybe, you could ride your bike through a sprinkler system! Step out of your comfort zone and go have fun! Just let it go. Take a little break. Let it be 5 minutes or 5 hours. It's all your choice. It's your journey, and this one moment in time could open a whole new opportunity for you. Go play!

Now, go have a great day with one thing in mind; jump, laugh, play. Go have some fun with the kid within.

You've got this!

Lots of Love & Tons of Light,

Vicki

Journal Entry: How did it feel to step out of your comfort zone and laugh a little more today? How can you add more of this to your life daily to keep it light and experience more joy and laughter in your life? Write about what it felt like to get in touch with the kid within.

Day 16: Your Daily Practice ∞

*"We learn to fly not be being fearless, but by
the daily practice of courage."*
~Sam Keen

You are just over the halfway mark of your 30-day commitment. Aren't you proud of yourself? You absolutely should be! They say it takes 30 days to change a habit, so I'd say you're off to a pretty damn good start. Hopefully, you've been working the program faithfully. If not, don't beat up on yourself but make a promise to stick to this book consistently for the next 15 days. Now, let's talk about how we're going to keep the focus on you and remain on track with your brand-new beginning. Keep in mind that once you find your toxic seed and remove it, you need to plant healthy seeds in its place. The exercises you've engaged in thus far have helped to plant new seeds in your garden of life. Your daily practice will nourish those seeds daily.

If you truly want to fuel your tank, you will need to be proactive. How you start your day is how you'll live your day, and how you end your day guides your tomorrow. If we don't start our day by fueling our tank, we are leaving a great deal to chance. If we don't end our day in a positive way, we are setting ourselves up for failure as we enter dreamland. It took me years to learn how important a daily practice was, but I will never let it go now that I have it. You see, people always say that motivation or positivity doesn't last. Truth is, neither does bathing or brushing your teeth, which is why we do that daily. Hence, if you want to stay motivated and on this path to healing, then you must create a daily practice for yourself. The only way to rid yourself of your core toxic belief is to re-teach, re-parent, and re-think.

What's A Daily Practice?

A daily practice is a routine that you will create for yourself to fuel your own tank. This practice will give you the power to take care of yourself and be your very best no matter what comes at you during the day. This is essentially the only way for you to stay the course and remain loyal to yourself.

Every morning is a new chance to begin again. Our minds can take us to some very dark and scary places. That's why we need to get ahead of that just as we open our eyes. I remember seeing Louise Hay speak years ago and she talked about the importance of how we start our day. She said that when she awoke in the morning she started with gratitude. She thanked her bed for a good night sleep, her home for protecting her, and her body for sustaining yet another day. There were many mornings when I was in my pit of hell that I would barely open my eyes and the tears were already filling up. These are the mornings that you don't even want to get out of bed. I knew at that moment that I had to do something. I had to create a daily practice that would not only help me get out of bed but inspire me to be my best throughout the day.

Here's what I do;

I wake up in the morning and set an intention for my day and say positive affirmations as you learned on Day 2. I do this even if my eyes are still closed and I'm saying them in my brain. If I am feeling anxious or sad, I like to say a mantra repeatedly that I learned in a meditation class years ago; *Om Namah Shivaya*. I was told this mantra would bring me peace and for some reason, it does. When I looked up the meaning online I found that this mantra is one of the most powerful for self-realization. As I've stated before, I am not religious. Instead, I am spiritual. If the shoe fits, I wear it. In other words, if it feels right I go with that, and this feels right to me, especially when I am feeling anxious or sad and in need of comfort. I then get out of bed (because by then my oldest dog is pawing at me or barking to go out). I make lunches for the day, get my son off to school, and go to my healing room/office to sit upon my meditation pillow. Some days, I pull an angel card. Other days, I read a short passage. I then close my eyes and do a brief mediation to center myself. Usually, clearing my chakras. Next, I head to the bathroom to do my mirror work, as you learned on Day 4. I am ready for the rest of the day. My day progresses and if I feel sad, disappointed, lost, or ready to jump in and save someone who doesn't want to be saved, I instead reach for my tools in my toolbox of life! At the end of the day, I always journal. Some nights, I like to journal about my day because I find writing cathartic and it helps me to process at a level that talking cannot. I journal with gratitude to remind myself of the blessings I have. Other nights, I read something positive (as I always have about 10 books on the nightstand) and then I journal about my reading. There you have it, my daily practice! I fuel myself by setting my intention as I'm opening my eyes, say positive affirmations, quiet my mind and center myself, look in the mirror and love the person staring back, use my tools throughout the day as needed, and then, I close my day on a positive note. This daily practice helps me to stay balanced. Some days are harder than others and I must reach for tools in that toolbox, but without a daily practice, I am lost at sea amid a frightening storm!

Today's Exercise:

Today, you will design *your* daily practice. You already have Day 2 and Day 4 that you should have been using consistently. If you haven't done that, then buckle up now and add that to your practice. Then, you just need to decide what else *feels* right for you. You might like to exercise in the morning or do yoga. You may have a book that's inspirational that you can read a short passage daily. Maybe you'll pull an angel card or some inspirational card and write a journal entry on it. Perhaps you enjoyed tapping and that might become part of your morning practice. It doesn't matter what you do. What matters most is that you do what fills your soul and brings you comfort and joy. Make sure that you have an activity or ritual you do consistently in the morning and then another one, or the same in the evening. Remember, how you start your day is how you live your day. And how you end your day, guides your tomorrow. You are in charge now. You can set intentions in your life, use your tools, and be your best-self daily – without rescuing others.

1) Start your day with your intentions and affirmations. Maybe, take some time to decide which affirmations are most important for you at this time to overcome a challenge.

2) Choose something to help clear and settle your mind; meditation, angel cards or some

inspirational cards, reading a passage from a positive book, yoga, exercise, tapping, etc.

3) Add in your mirror work. Again, if you are focused on overcoming a challenge, be sure to make those affirmations focus on this area to give you the empowerment you need to cross this bridge.

4) Use the tools you've learned thus far in the book to keep you on track throughout the day. The moment you feel like you are dangerously close to a rabbit hole, reach for your toolbox. You've got this!

5) Decide how to best serve yourself as you close your day; journaling, writing, yoga, exercise, reading, etc.

Know that this practice you create is a practice that you are going to have for the rest of your life. You can change the elements of the practice, but *this is your time to care for yourself* and it's critical to not only burn the damn cape, but live a happy, healthy life.

Please note that when things start going great for you – and they will – you mustn't eliminate the daily practice. If you do (and I know you might because I did too), you will only begin falling into those holes once again. This time is for you. A time to be proactive and fuel your soul with the positive energy that you need to not only remove your core toxic belief, but to begin again with healthy seeds in your garden of life.

Now, go have a great day with one thing in mind; your daily practice is your time for you. Understand, it must be completed *daily* to fill your tank. You owe this to yourself.

You've got this!

Lots of Love & Tons of Light,

Vicki

Journal Entry: How do I feel having a daily practice where I am setting aside time for just me? What are the obstacles that might hold me back from my daily practice? How can I proactively problem solve to avoid abandoning this critical practice for myself?

∞ I know you haven't seen this symbol in a while but don't forget it means *daily*. It's part of your new routine to fuel your soul, heal, and burn that damn cape!

Day 17: Be Your Own Best Friend ∞

*"We have to learn to be our own best friend
because we fall too easily into the trap of
being our own worst enemy."*
~Roderick Thorp

It's good to have friends. Friends can lift you up when you're feeling down. They can give you a sense of community and show you parts of yourself that you never knew existed. They will laugh with you, cry with you, hell, some might even die for you! A best friend, awe, now that's something very special. A best friend is that person who's been there for you through thick and thin. They've seen you rise to your very best and watched you fall to your extreme worst. They've grown with you, held your head up when you felt like you couldn't, and they support you in any way they can. A best friend is that one person who you know you can always depend on. But what if they fall out of love with you? What if they move to another country? What if they have their own life that gets bumpy, consumes them, and they become distant? Worse yet, what if you don't have that one person who is always there for you? It can be very lonely to feel like you're in the world all alone and no-one truly cares for you, but that's just another lie you tell yourself when your toxic belief is at the helm of your ship.

When I was going through my dark era, I'm quite sure my friends no longer wanted to hear about Richard. They didn't like him from the beginning and they just wanted me to let go and move on. I, however, felt that I needed to understand why he couldn't be the person I wanted him to be – the person he advertised to me. I was up and down with this guy for so long that even though my friends would look me right in the eye when I spoke, I could sense the eye roll they were holding back. It was painful. I got to a point where I didn't want to talk about my emotional distress anymore because; 1) It was clear my friends didn't want to hear it, 2) I was disgusted by it, and 3) Talking about it wasn't making it any better. I began to isolate myself. I didn't want to go anywhere or do anything because I felt that no-one understood me or truly wanted to be near me because I was so damn negative. This is when I had to look deep into that mirror. You see, because I had pushed away even those who did truly care about me, I had only one person to depend on, and that was the woman staring back at me in the mirror. But don't feel bad for me, because honestly, that was the best thing that could've ever happened for me. Sadly, I had gotten to that point of wanting someone else to rescue me. I was constantly searching for the wisdom to heal outside of myself. I was looking for others to lift me up and give me the answers I so deeply desired. Yet even when I'd get an answer, I didn't like it. I feel truly blessed that I got to the point where I felt like I had no-one to truly lean on, because it was there that I realized I had myself, and that was all I truly needed!

You've Got This!

It's great to have friends. It's even more amazing to have a best friend, but let's be real with ourselves, no-one can *always* be there for you. Everyone's got their own shit they're dealing with and the raw truth is that your power grows exponentially when you know you can depend on yourself. There's going to come a time when you are crying in the middle of the night or in need of assistance at a time when others simply won't be there for you and you will need to be there for yourself. This may seem like the darkest time of your life, but trust me, it's a gift. I remember feeling so alone that I thought I would die; there was no-one there who wanted to listen and even when they did listen, nothing made the pain any better. The only person who could make me feel better in my darkest hour, was me. I had to learn how to comfort, boost, praise, empower, and love myself. I had to be there for me. Truth is, when push comes to shove, no-one is going to love you and protect you like you are. It's just a simple fact. Don't abandon your friends but start realizing that you don't *need* anyone else. It's okay to *want* people in your life, but understand that you don't need them. You have everything that you need, and more!

A best friend knows you inside and out, right? Well, who the hell knows you better than yourself? No-one. Not even your best friend. You know deep down what you need, want, and desire. You just need to get out of your own way and be the friend you need when others aren't available (or even when they are). Know your worth. Know that you matter and that you've literally got this.

I believe we all need someone to lean on, but you don't want to lean so hard that you knock them over. If you can learn to be your own best friend, then your relationships with others will improve vastly because you won't be so needy. We become needy when we feel that we are broken and in need of repair. We seek advice and help in any way we can get it when we are at our darkest hour. We begin to drain others in the same way that we often feel drained by our 'object of affection.' Our people (friends and family) feel drained because they *can't* help us. They don't have what we need to feel better. Only we have the antidote, and that's self-love.

Becoming your own best friend also means not beating up on yourself. We can be our own worst enemy at times. You now have tools that you've worked on. Use those tools to your advantage. Take care of yourself like you've taken care of everyone else in the years leading up to this very moment. Speak kindly to yourself, always give yourself the support you need – even if that means reaching out to a professional, stand up for yourself, listen to what you truly need, want, and desire, set clear boundaries with expectations that you know you'll follow through on, and see yourself as perfect *just as you are*. Know that you are perfectly imperfect, and that's the beauty of the person you see staring back in the mirror. We all make mistakes in life. We all have a knack for certain things and suck at others. It's all perfect just as it is. Love yourself for the bad, the good, and the indifferent just like you have loved your best friend, your husband, your wife, your partner, your children, and the guy next door. Be there for **you** first, and the rest will fall into place.

Today's Exercise:

1) *Beware of your mind*: We know that the mind can take us to some very dark places. Begin your day by being an observer of your thoughts about you. If you think poorly of yourself, it's going to be difficult to love yourself. Go through your morning daily practice and when you look in the mirror, really look deep into your own eyes and see the beauty deep within you. When a negative thought comes up about yourself during the day, use one of the tools you've learned so far to help you turn that thought around and accept yourself in this very moment for who you are.

Ex) *I overthink and that leads to trouble in my life.*

a) Tap it out: Even though I tend to overthink things in life, I still deeply and completely love and approve of myself – then go through the tapping points; my mind is racing but I know I can get through this, I don't have to know everything that is happening right now, I know I can handle just about anything, I can slow down my thoughts and remind myself that I am safe, I am lovable, I am worthy, I am enough or I am important. It's okay to overthink sometimes, as long as I can bring myself back to center, overthinking is not serving me, it's sabotaging me. I choose to focus on the good and know that all is well and happening in Divine order.

b) MIRROR:

Recognize – I am aware that I overthink things in life and it leads me down a road of turmoil.

Realize – I can choose to keep thinking this way and feeling terrible about myself, or I can turn these thoughts around because it doesn't feel good to think this way. It does not serve me.

Respond – I take action by using thought stopping and then turning the thought around. My new thought is, "I am right here, right now, in this moment. I have no control over the future. I am present in the now and all is well."

c) Journaling: Grab your journal and write that shit out! I've spoken about this a few times in the book. Best friends serve as a terrific sounding board. Be your own best friend and talk yourself off the ledge by journaling your thoughts and feelings. Works like a charm every time for me!

2) *Treat yourself with kindness today (and every day forward).* When you feel unbalanced, take the time to do whatever it is that you need to rebalance yourself. Don't depend on anyone else to lift you up. Know that you've got this. You own your power and you have all that you need to put sunshine back in your heart when you're feeling gloomy. Say kind words and do kind acts for you, yourself and you!

3) *Laugh a little.* Find a way to get in touch with that little kid within throughout your day. Remember who you are in all your essence. You are not a slave to your circumstances. You are here to enjoy life and live life. You are not here to exist through life.

4) *Give yourself a kick in the ass (as needed).* Best friends don't let us stay down for too long. Use the 80:20 rule. Don't allow negative energy to overwhelm your day and your life.

5) *Take care of your body.* Listen to your body. Listen for what it needs, wants and desires and answer the call. If you need to rest, then rest. If you need nourishment, then nourish yourself. If you need chocolate, then indulge. If you need to move, then move. Listen and answer the call.

Now, go have a great day with one thing in mind; be your own best friend.

You've got this!

Lots of Love & Tons of Light,

Vicki

Journal Entry: How does it feel to know that I can take care of myself on every level; mind, body and spirit? What can I do to remind myself that I don't *need* anyone else if I truly have me? Journal about your overall feelings this evening.

Day 18: Celebrate Your Wins ∞

*"My whole teaching is this; accept yourself,
love yourself, & celebrate yourself."*
~Osho

Do you celebrate your wins? Do you give yourself credit where credit is due? Rescuers are damn hard on themselves. They are problem solvers. They know how to make things happen. They don't usually panic in the face of disaster because they started formulating a plan the moment they saw shit rolling downhill. They are proactive. They size up a situation in minutes and don't hesitate to jump in and solve a problem, no matter where they are or when it happens. This gives them the idea that they *should* have all the answers. Consequently, when the shit hits the fan in *their* lives, they are frustrated when they can't fix a situation – even if it has nothing to do with them because the other person is unwilling to grow or change. It's true! Think about your life. Are you hard on yourself? Do you have unfair expectations of yourself and possibly others? Are you quick to find your flaws even when you are being complimented? There's something to be said for looking at oneself and always wanting to do more, but you cross the line of self-love when you are constantly finding the negative and almost never acknowledging the positive. That's why today, you're going to learn to celebrate your wins.

The Glass is Half Full

When you wake up late and you feel like you're behind the eight ball, you're quick to point this out to yourself and create more negative thoughts. How about turning that around? If you're running late and you get yourself out the door (the animals are fed, the house is still standing, and the kids are taken care of), give yourself the credit you deserve. Small, daily victories still deserve notice. When you've worked hard on a project, it's the end of your commitment and you've finished, praise yourself. Maybe there's no-one else who notices your hard work, but why shouldn't you? Celebrate your wins. There are many more triumphs than you care to admit. Every day you multitask like nobody's business. You keep the household afloat and you balance the day-to-day functions. You deserve a pat on the back. We focus on what still needs to be done too much and don't give ourselves credit for what we've already accomplished. Remember when you were a little kid and you completed a task and couldn't wait to ask the adult what they thought? Well, instead of waiting for someone else to praise you, give yourself the positive feedback that you want, need, and so deserve! Put the focus on the half of the glass that is full instead of the half that has yet to be filled.

We go through our day putting out many fires, yet we never pause to say, 'good job!' It's not selfish to stop, self-reflect, and give yourself praise. Instead (I've said it before and I'll say it again), it's self-care. Part of loving yourself is learning to give yourself the praise that you never got as a child and still seek as an adult. Do you remember the story I shared where I told you when my 1st graders come to me looking for approval, I get down on their level and ask, "What do you think?" I do that because I want them to approve of themselves first. After they share their own pride in their work, I give them a compliment. However, what is most important to me is that they learn to feel proud of themselves first. You're going to do the same today. We are still seeking that approval that we sought as children, whether we care to realize this or not. Be mindful of yourself today. Give yourself the credit that is due and you'll feel a whole lot better by the end of your day!

Today you will praise yourself for every little win that comes your way. No win is too small for recognition;

- You got to work on time.

- Your kid is doing well in school.

- You navigated a trying situation with ease.

- You completed a project you've worked on for a long time.

- Someone you helped along the way is feeling successful.

- The law of Karma came through in a relationship for you.

- You're a hard worker.

- You got all the green lights.

- Your body is healthy.

- It's gloomy out, but you feel sunshiny on the inside.

- You completed your daily practice today.

- Instead of jumping in to save someone today, you sat back and just listened.

- You are being mindful.

- When you started to feel overwhelmed, you used your new tools instead and turned that shit around.

- You spoke up for yourself today.

- You finally said, "No" to a project you didn't need to be involved in.

- You are serving yourself instead of sabotaging yourself in a situation.

- You feel worthy, important, safe, lovable, or enough!

Today's Exercise:

1) Before you leave your home today, take out your journal and list 5 things that you've accomplished in the past 5 days.

2) In the middle of the day, reflect on 5 things that you've accomplished so far in your day (yes, it can be the simple events like getting to work on time).

3) In the evening, list 10 things that you've accomplished over the course of your life!

Now, go have a great day with one thing in mind; give yourself credit where credit is due and celebrate your wins.

You've got this!

Lots of Love & Tons of Light,

Vicki

Journal Entry: See above and then journal how it feels to recognize your greatness.

*If you are a member on the website www.vickisavini. com/member, click Day 18 for a worksheet and video on celebrating your wins.

Day 19: Respond Instead of Reacting

∞

"When you start responding instead of reacting to life, life will start responding to you."
~Jim Rohn

You've spent your entire life putting others first, seeking approval outside of yourself and solving everyone else's problems. You've given too much, opened yourself up to extreme vulnerability, and handed your power over countless times. Let's be honest, you've been taken advantage of a great deal in your life. It's therefore easy for you to believe that people are 'out to get you.' You've always been the strong one and have taken care of everything in most situations. That makes it difficult for you to trust others. Some might call you controlling. You're not truly controlling, but you *are* fearful. You are fearful that if you don't have a plan, everything will fall apart. Reacting to life is fear based. There is a fear at the core that you are going to be damaged in some way. You are therefore driven by fear and giving your power away. When something appears to be going wrong, your first go-to might be more reactive than responsive, and who could blame you? Responding to life is staying in control of your emotions and coming from a place of love. When you react to life it is as if you are having a knee jerk reaction. Instead of taking it in and looking at the whole picture, you emotionally spring into action. As soon as a spark flies, you grab the fire extinguisher and run towards the fire. But sometimes, that's not your best option. Granted, there are plenty of instances when you need to douse a fire as quickly as possible, but there's always time to step back, evaluate the situation, and then respond. Patience, young grasshopper. When we respond to life, we remain in control. Instead of reacting in an emotional means, we stop, take a breath and then move forward to put the fire out. There are times when sparks fly and a fire never ignites. However, when we react we are jumping to conclusions, and we sometimes ignite a fire that was never going to become a full blaze.

Don't Take It Personally

How many times have you jumped into action and reacted to a situation because at the core, you were personally offended? I'm sure if you step back, breathe, and look at these situations mindfully, you will quickly see that you were taking something personally. This isn't uncommon because – as rescuers – we have high expectations of ourselves and everyone around us. Sometimes, we can be a bit perfectionistic. Of course, this relates back to our toxic core beliefs. Therefore, the good news is, we can in fact shift this behavior and begin to respond instead of reacting to life.

This might sound a bit harsh, but it's not always about you. You are a passionate and loving individual but when you are seeking approval or trying to prove yourself to others, you lack the ability to separate yourself from the situation. I pride myself on being extremely communicative with parents of students in my classroom and I strive to empower my students every step of the way. I ask my students to evaluate their behavior and class participation weekly on a sheet I call the 'weekly round up.' One half of this sheet has questions in kid language and the kids evaluate themselves. The kids are asked to think about their behavior and participation throughout the week and fill their side out honestly. I then collect the papers and fill in my half of the sheet that has similar questions in adult lingo. If there is a discrepancy, then the student and I meet privately to discuss. I have done this for years because I don't feel it's beneficial for adults to tell kids about their behavior and hand down a punishment without self-reflection and accountability. Without self-reflection and accountability kids will continue to seek your approval and do what's right *mostly* when you're looking. By choosing to do the weekly round up in this fashion, I feel strongly that kids are held accountable for their behavior because they are aware that I am going to fill in my side after them, we will discuss if needed, and then the page goes home to their parents. One year, I had a parent question whether this method was positive reinforcement because their child was not listening and following directions. I tried to communicate with the parent several times about their child's behavior, but they were in complete denial, even though I had several complaints from other teachers and substitutes who had been in my room in my absence. When I first received communication about their concern, I was offended. I was offended because I am very mindful of my students and always strive to empower them and teach them to be accountable to themselves. I wanted to fire back correspondence as soon as I saw the email come in. However, instead of reacting, I closed the email and stepped back. I began to look at the full picture and decided it was best to invite the child and parents in for a discussion so there were no misunderstandings through email. Whew! That was much better than firing back an emotional email because I was offended. It was more responsive to take a breath and open the conversation for discussion. I could then explain the premise of the weekly round-up once again to the parents and work together to help their child to understand the importance of self-reflection and accountability.

The Sky Isn't Falling

Most situations that we face daily are not complete emergencies. We make them emergencies due to our fear and the triggers of our core toxic belief. We could give ourselves some breathing room and begin to respond instead of reacting to life by simply taking a step back and prioritizing the situation. Just because you get an email or text message, doesn't mean you need to respond immediately. Take the time to stand back and gain a deeper perspective so you are not taking it personally. Remind yourself that it's not always about you and that you haven't failed. Walk away from the situation for a bit to gain some insight and then come back and respond instead of reacting out of pure emotion. Yes, there are going to be times when you will need to respond quickly, but keep in mind that there's always time to step back, breathe, and then respond without the attached emotion. You will feel a whole lot better when you respond to life instead of reacting because you are not giving your power away. Hold onto your power. Instead of thinking people are out to get you, get all the facts and then respond.

Today's Exercise:

When we are in the midst of chaos we react quickly to survive. In today's exercise you will practice patience – often a difficult task for a rescuer. You are always in 'go-mode.' Today, when situations pop up, you are going to stop, breathe, remind yourself that this is not an emergency and then respond. This could be anything from someone sending a text message to you and not diving for your phone to a person verbally attacking you for no apparent reason.

1) Think of an instance when you reacted to a situation instead of responding.

_____

_____

_____

2) How did that work out for you?

_____

_____

_____

3) What additional issues surfaced because you were quick to charge the fire instead of breathing and evaluating first?

_____

_____

_____

4) Say this phrase three times: *This too shall pass*

I get it, when the shit hits the fan, you want to charge right out there with a quick plan, but today, we're going to harness that energy a bit. When something comes up for you today and you feel like your emotions are throwing you into the fire, stop, breathe, then say, "This too shall pass." It always seems much worse than it is when we are in the middle of the fire.

5) Take a step back and gain a broader perspective.

Remember, not everything is directly related to you (you may feel blamed, like you're being held accountable or feeling insufficient). See how this situation relates back to your core toxic belief and then *use your tools* (Mirror process, affirmations, mindfulness, etc.) to pause for a moment so you can hold onto your power and respond. When the adrenaline has lessened, go back to solve the problem.

Now, go have a great day with one thing in mind; respond instead of reacting.

You've got this!

Lots of Love & Tons of Light,

Vicki

Journal Entry: Reflect on how it feels when you react to life. Then reflect on how it feels to respond to life. How can you center yourself in the midst of feeling attacked to hold onto your power and respond?

Day 20: Deactivate Your Triggers

"A trigger is anything that sets you off emotionally and activates memories of your trauma."

~Jasmin Lee Cori

We all have triggers that activate our original trauma. Whatever it was that planted the seed long ago is engaged whenever a whiff of that experience arises. This is when we become driven by fear instead of love. We go into fight or flight mode and become extremely defensive. This explains what we learned in the last chapter about taking life personally. Something triggers us and starts the download once again that we are; not enough, not worthy, not safe, not lovable, or not important. Knowing your triggers are a huge factor to your healing. It is once again that first step in the MIRROR process – awareness. Once you are aware, you can see that you have alternatives and take a different course of action. Up to this point in your life you have been triggered repeatedly, but you were unaware. This made it easy to fall into those damn rabbit holes without an understanding of why. Today's lesson on loving yourself is focused on revealing your triggers so you can deactivate those little bastards and hold onto your power.

Most people can't remember life when they were an infant or toddler. My mom was always vastly amazed by what I recalled from early childhood. While I was working with a therapist on healing my inner child, I was able to clearly see myself in a playpen watching my sisters and mother engage in life while I felt invisible. I can still feel that pain of invisibility. Everyone was going about their business and doing their own thing while I stood in that playpen hoping to be noticed and connected with. That is my earliest memory of not feeling important. There are several others that I've worked through over the years. Yet, no matter how much work I do to heal these memories, the imprint is still left there in my mind and heart; I am not important. It has taken me years to learn my triggers. At this point in my life, I am clear on those triggers and I have tools to help me to move beyond them when they arise, and yes, they still arise. As you know, my core toxic belief is; I'm not important. When I feel ignored or invisible in some way, I am activated. What does that mean? It means that I become anxious, defensive, angry, paranoid, and sometimes depressed. My heart begins to beat faster, my breathing becomes shallow and the hair raises on my arms. Sometimes I can feel the heat rising within my body. I'm in attack mode. Because I've been triggered, my mind goes to a very dark place. I brace myself and go into overprotective mode, protecting myself from everyone and everything. When I am in this place I believe that I am alone, no-one truly cares for me, and that everyone is out to get me. At times, I can convince myself that I will never truly be happy because I am not important, and therefore, I don't matter. This is all in my mind. My subconscious mind created this long ago as a reactive response to life to somehow protect me, but we can all see that this is false. I have come to learn that my triggers involve anything that have to do with feeling ignored, dismissed, or pushed aside. In the past if I sent an email and it was not answered for days, it would infuriate me. Same with a text message or phone call. If I reached out to a friend and didn't hear back, I immediately took it personally. I now know when I am triggered, and I use the steps in today's exercise to talk myself away from reactive measures.

On the bright side, I am mindfully aware of everyone around me and keenly aware of those who feel invisible. It's critically important to me that people feel seen and heard because of my own triggers, and perhaps that's made me a better person. I am therefore thankful for the insight and hopeful that once you find your triggers, you too can use the tools to respond instead of reacting when you are activated. My triggers have given me the opportunity to heal and be a better person. Perhaps you'll feel the same someday.

Today's Exercise:

This exercise begins with a meditation. You can record your voice, have someone read it to you or go to the membership site; www.vickisavini.com/member

Get yourself into a relaxed position. Close your eyes and take a long deep breath in through your nose. Release slowly through your mouth. Breathe in again and release. As you continue to breathe in through your nose and release through your mouth, allow your body to completely relax, letting go of all thoughts and tension. Continue breathing, in through the nose and out through the mouth. Now, imagine yourself standing at the top of a white staircase. You are an adult. Breathe in and as you release take a step down. With each new breath step down one more stair. As you step down the stairs, imagine yourself getting younger and younger. When you see yourself as a teen, stop and take a few breaths. Say your toxic core belief out loud, then slowly descend the staircase. As you step down go back to one memory at a time during your youth when your toxic core belief was validated. When you get to a vivid memory, stop on that stair and breathe in and out slowly for three long breaths. What triggered you? What makes you feel unworthy, not enough, unimportant, unlovable, or unsafe? Breathe in and release that out. Hold onto this feeling and open your eyes.

Fill out the following or grab the pdf on the member site.

My core toxic belief is: _____
_____

I remember when I was _____ years old.

Tell about the memory;

Who was there? _____
_____

What was said? _____
_____

How does this connect to your life now?

Relate this to situations in your life as an adult (thinking back to my example of being in the playpen for long periods of time and feeling ignored).

On the lines below, write the situations or actions that trigger you.

I am triggered (anxious, upset, sad, angry) when

_____

This relates to: _____
_____
_____
_____

Cause: In the oval, write the trigger (ex. People ignoring my emails, texts, etc.) This is what causes angst for you.

Effect: On the lines connecting from the oval, write the feelings or reactions that occur from this trigger. (I panic, get very anxious, lash out at people, send nasty emails, become needy)

img4

When you are triggered, you need to reach for one (or several) of the tools you've learned so far;

> MIRROR process

> Affirmations

> Mindful Moment

> Mirror Work

> Tapping

> Journaling

*One tool may or may not work for you. Remember these are beliefs that have been held for a very long time. I recommend turning the thought around with tapping, then using affirmations while looking in a mirror if you are in deep panic. Journaling can also be helpful during dire straits. Use the tool that feels right to you and allow yourself to shift your focus back to you and the current moment reminding yourself that you are safe, important, worthy, lovable or enough.

Now, go have a great day with one thing in mind; deactivate those triggers and remind yourself it all starts in your mind.

You've got this!

Lots of Love & Tons of Light,

Vicki

Journal Entry: Take some time this evening to journal about triggers that may have come up for you throughout the day that validated that toxic belief. If you didn't have any triggers come up, then journal how it feels to be driven by love instead of fear.

Day 21: Protect Your Energy ∞

"Spend time with people who are good for
your mental health."
~Idil Ahmed

They say that you are the average of the five people you spend the most time with. Hmmmmm, that's something to think about! We are energetic beings who thrive on connection. Just like animals, we feel the energy of others even when they are miles away from us. Have you ever noticed how spending time with some people inspires and energizes you, while others drain the shit out of you? The people we choose to associate with can have a massive impact on our well-being. You have been working so hard to heal your toxic core belief and build your self-worth, the last thing you need is an energy vampire!

Energy vampires suck the life out of you. They are emotionally immature people who truly believe the whole world revolves around them. They can drain you mentally, physically, emotionally and financially, if you allow it. It may be that friend that is forever disappointed with life and wants advice, but never does follow through with anything to change their circumstances. You listen to their 'woe is me' story each time you get together, and you try to be a good friend and listen. You can't get a word in edgewise, anyways. You want to say, "chill the hell out!" but you refrain because you don't want to hurt their feelings. You leave the meeting feeling drained every time. Perhaps, it's not that friend, but instead that person in your life who is so needy that every conversation is about them. They might be the drama queen or the know-it-all. It gets more difficult to be around them as the time capacity expands. Maybe they don't get out enough or they can't see the trees through the forest, but nonetheless, you walk away feeling drained every single time. Then there's the extreme energy vampire. Sadly, this person is usually your object of affection. They drain your mind, body, and spirit because you've allowed yourself to be consumed with fixing and healing them instead of keeping the focus on you. No more! Hold the stop sign up with blazing red lights. A critical part of loving yourself and being your own hero is spending more time with people who energize and inspire you and distancing yourself from those who drain you. You are a work in progress. If you truly love yourself, you won't subject yourself to energy vampires.

Your Closest Circle

Who are the people in your closest circle? Right now, stop, close your eyes and imagine the top five people you spend most of your time with. Do they energize you? Do they inspire you? Do they make you feel loved, safe, and fully supported? Do you laugh together? Can they accept you for the bad, good, and indifferent? As you grow and change, the people you associate yourself with will also need to grow and change. Otherwise, you will not be able to flourish because you are subjecting yourself to toxic situations and people. Spend your time with people who energize and inspire you. The more time you spend with those who validate your negative core toxic belief, the slower your healing process is. Go out and have great conversations. Laugh a little more. Dream a little more. Fill your tank with positive energy from the people you choose to surround yourself with. You will inevitably have to spend time with some of those energy vampires. Maybe you're related to them or you work for them, so you must proactively arm yourself with positive energy from your tribe. You may be realizing that you need a whole new tribe (your closest circle). Spend most of your time with those who add something positive to your energy and limit your time with those who drain your energy.

Dealing with Energy Vampires

It's clear that you should surround yourself with those who inspire you, but you are inevitably going to be forced to deal with energy vampires at times. So how the hell do you do that while still holding onto your power and putting yourself first?

1) **Be aware**. Once you know who the people are who drain your energy, you can proactively gear yourself up before spending time with them. I had a client who would get anxious and ornery whenever she needed to spend time with her family. More specifically, her mom. She knew that no matter how much healing she did with me, her mother was still going to demean her because she wasn't healing herself. We would meet prior to the visit to build her confidence, remind her who she truly was, and go over the following steps.

2) **Protect yourself**. Make sure you keep yourself safe by placing yourself in an imaginary bubble while you are in their company. Constantly remind yourself that you can choose a different path now. Set your intention, say your affirmations and use your tools. Know that you have boundary lines and don't allow anyone to cross them.

3) **Respond instead of reacting**. Allow them to talk, as they will anyway, and instead of engaging them or reacting to them when they are baiting you

just keep reminding yourself that it's not about you, it's about them. While they are going on and on continue rehearsing your new positive belief (the opposite of your toxic belief) in your mind. If you feel attacked, take a deep breath and bite down so you can think before you respond. It's not necessarily what you say, but rather how you say it to an energy vampire that makes the difference. Many times, they just like to listen to themselves talk, so let them talk and focus on your positive affirmations. Tomorrow, you will learn how to speak your truth. That might also come in handy with these energy vampires.

4) *Lower your expectations*. Zebras don't lose their stripes. Lower your expectations. See them for who they are and not for who you want them to be. Don't expect them to be anything other than who they've always been to you. Stand back, breathe, respond, and release. If you need to cut your time short because it's too draining, then go ahead. Never betray yourself.

5) *Limit your time in their presence*. Okay, so you might have to be around some of these people who drain the shit out of your energy but limit your time with them. Always have another place to be or something else to do (even if it's washing your hair). There's nothing wrong with you spending short periods of time with them

and then stepping away. This is true even if it's a colleague or boss you work for. Get in and get out. What's the task? How would you like it completed? Then, out!

6) **Cut them out**. If you've gotten to a point where you cannot be around this person without being deeply affected, *then you must cut them out of your life*. Sadly, it doesn't matter if it's a person you thought was the love of your life or a family member. Love yourself first. Be firm and honest. Set those clear boundaries with consequences, and if they can't be around you without crossing your boundaries, then they don't deserve you in their lives. It's that simple. Let go of the guilt and do what you must to serve yourself. If they won't change and you can no longer tolerate them, then they simply must go! (Check out a helpful video on this at the member site listed under Day 21 www.vickisavini.com/member)

Today's Exercise:

List the top 5 people you spend the most time with:

1) _____

   _____

2) _____

   _____

3) _____

   _____

4) _____

   _____

5) _____

   _____

Look at that list and write a + sign if they energize or inspire you and a − if they drain you.

Now, next to their name, write how they energize, inspire, or drain you.

How's your list looking? If it's true that the top five people you spend your time with is the average of you, then do you like how this weighs out? If any of the people on your list drain you, then you might want to replace them with someone who inspires or energizes you. You might, if you'd truly like to burn the damn cape and be your own hero. Just sayin'.

If you don't have five people you spend the most time with who inspire you, then it's time to look for new tribe members. Remember, we are energetically sensitive beings who long for connection. Spending large amounts of time with energy vampires will only sabotage you. It will take your joy away and drain your energy. Don't let anyone steal your joy!

Now, go have a great day with one thing in mind; spend time with those who energize and inspire you.

You've got this!

Lots of Love & Tons of Light,

Vicki

Journal Entry: Who are the people you need to spend more time with? How will this benefit you? Who are the people you need to distance yourself from? How will that benefit you? Is there anyone you need to cut out of your life? What would your life be like without the stress from this person?

Day 22: Speak Your Truth

"Speak your truth, even if your voice shakes."
~ Robin Sharma

You've always been a bit of a people pleaser. You're the kind one who always wants to take care of everyone else. You want to be sure everyone feels at ease and is comfortable in the situation. How may I serve, right? You don't want to put anyone in a bad spot or make them feel uncomfortable. God forbid they get pissed off and argue with you. That's the worst! You're proactive. You don't want to fight. You might try to put yourself in their shoes to understand what's happening, instead of taking care of your own needs. Then of course, there is that fear that they will get angry and no longer engage in the relationship or they'll somehow make life hell for you. Sure, you've tried to tell people how you feel. You've dropped hints and stated that you were frustrated but the moment they chimed in with their side of the story, you stepped back and imagined their perspective. Once you were able to see their side, you suddenly felt a bit foolish for asking for your needs to be met. Let's not rock the boat. Rescuers don't like conflict. They like to keep the peace and smooth everything out, so everyone is happy. Everyone, except for the rescuer. Does this sound at all familiar?

When you're of this mindset and a need of your own is not being met, it's often difficult to speak up for yourself. However, if you truly want to love yourself and be your own hero, then you really need to 'speak your truth, even when your voice shakes.' I have been dying to write that quote through this entire journey. It's one of my favorite quotes because it has given me strength in some of the most difficult seasons of my life. What does that mean, speak your truth? I just love the sound of that. It means that you speak what's deep inside of you – the absolute truth you feel – instead of sugar-coating shit to take care of others. Believe it or not, this is what you're going to learn. But don't worry, I'm going to rev you up first!

Stand Tall & Be Firm

In the summers, I run camps to empower kids to believe in themselves and speak their truth. One of the exercises that we created years ago after teaching mirror work was what we like to call *power yoga*. We take affirmations and speak them aloud with poses to reflect the feeling you have while in this pose. I use power yoga in my classroom as well. One pose we put affirmations to was *child pose*. For this pose, the kids curl up in a ball on the floor with knees out like a frog and head to the mat and they give themselves a hug. They then say, "I am whole. I am perfect. I am complete." Another pose we use is *tree pose*. As the kids bring one leg up and balance on their opposite leg, they say, "I am focused. I am balanced. I am strong." My all-time favorite and most powerful is *mountain pose*. Kids stand with their feet shoulder width apart and arms at their sides. I ask them to stand tall and plant their feet firmly in the ground feeling their strength and power. I tell them to stand firm because I am coming around the room to gently push on their shoulder to see if they actually believe in themselves, or if they will push over easily. I then ask them to close their eyes and repeat after me, "I am a mountain. Nothing and no-one can knock me down. I am strong. I am powerful. I believe in myself. I am confident." The power in that room is unbelievable! We've run a specific camp for girls for about 10 years now. A few years back one of our previous campers came to us as a teenager and told us a story about when she was being bullied in 9th grade. She said it was awful. She was afraid to go to her locker every day because she knew the mean girls were going to be there and they would heckle her and throw things at her. As I was listening to her, I started to tear up. She smiled and said, "No, Ms. Savini, it's okay. I finally stood up for myself. I kept thinking about mountain pose and said the words to myself all the way down the hall, and by the time I got to my locker, I stuck up for myself. I used a firm 'I statement' and told them they didn't scare me anymore. They stopped within a few days. I guess they got bored!" From that point forward, I had a whole different view of power yoga and mountain pose. I even began to use this strategy for myself and in workshops with adults. I used it to get through my divorce, to find the courage to speak my truth with Dick, and to deal with situations where I must confront others.

*For fun, go to the Mindful Teacher page on Facebook, and click this link; https://bit.ly/2K7P9jU. It's a video of a small group of girls at one of our camps demonstrating mountain pose.

There's something to be said about standing firm, in your power and speaking with confidence. I must have thousands of children and adults who use that currently because I teach it wherever I go. Now it's your turn.

Right now, go and stand in front of a mirror. Stand with your feet shoulder width apart. Roll your shoulders back and straighten your spine. Pretend there's a string at the crown of your head pulling you up as tall as you can be. Stand firm. Feel the strength in your legs and the power in your back. You are supported. Now, look straight ahead into the mirror and say, "I am a mountain. Nothing and no-one can knock me down. I am strong. I am powerful. I believe in myself. I am confident." Didn't quite believe it? Maybe your voice was a little soft? Let's try that again. Stand tall and firmly say, "I am a mountain. Nothing and no-one can knock me down. I am strong. I am powerful. I believe in myself. I am confident." Any better? Did you believe it more this time? If not, go at it again and again until you can feel the power. This is a great exercise to add into your daily practice, especially as you are learning to speak your truth.

Speak Your Truth

It is not always easy to speak your truth. There are many factors that go into speaking your truth. First, you must be sure of your truth. Then, you must get over your fears. Finally, you must have the courage to speak up, set a boundary and follow through. In my camps, classroom, and workshops, I teach children and adults to speak their truth by using an 'I Statement.' I can't take credit for this, as it's been around for a very long time, but I can tell you it works. It works for 6-year-olds and it works for 60-year-olds as well! Here's the format of the 'I Statement.'

I feel _____
_____

(tell what you are feeling; sad, disappointed, discouraged, lonely, etc.)

When _____
_____

(tell when you feel this way)

Because _____
_____

(tell why you feel this way, what is happening to cause the above feeling)

What I Really Need is _____
_____
_____

(be clear about what you need from the other person)

Example: (to use when you are asking for someone else to make a change or honor a boundary)

I feel <u>angry</u>

When <u>you ignore my requests to stop playing with your phone and pay attention to me</u>

Because <u>I am important</u>

What I really need is <u>for you to please put the phone down and spend time with me or I am no longer sitting here with you.</u>

Example: (to use when you realize that the other person isn't going to change and you need to take care of yourself)

I feel <u>frustrated in this relationship</u>

When <u>he lies to me and ignores my needs</u>

Because <u>I deserve better</u>

What I really need <u>is to take care of myself and get the hell out of this relationship!</u>

Ta da!

Today's Exercise:

1) Sit down and write an 'I Statement' to someone that you would like to confront.

2) Stand in front of the mirror and say, "I am a mountain. Nothing and no-one can knock me down. I am strong. I am powerful. I am confident. I believe in myself." Then continue to say the words you remember from that phrase in your mind until you get to the person you need to speak with.

3) Go speak your truth. Yes, even if your voice shakes!

Now, go have a great day with one thing in mind; stand tall and speak firmly.

You've got this!

Lots of Love & Tons of Light,

Vicki

Journal Entry: What are some other 'I Statements' you might want to consider using to set some boundaries and honor yourself? Write a few 'I statements' including some that are just for you and not necessarily to confront another person. How do you feel when you are in mountain pose reciting the phrase?

Day 23: Trust Yourself, The Answers are Within ∞

"The best place to find a helping hand is at the end of your own arm."
~Swedish Proverb

You may not know this yet, but the answers you seek to all your problems are deep within you. You have gone to other sources for many years because that's what you were taught to do. You were taught to ask others for their opinion and depend on others to give you the information you needed to make decisions. Years ago, if you didn't know the answer you sought out a professional in that area. Today, you hop on the internet and Google is your friend. Sure, we can seek all kinds of information out there, whether it be from one person to another or through research, but the best knowledge comes from within. It is deep within that you will always discover your truth. Sounds very Obi-Wan-*ish*, right? It seems like that should've been a Star Wars quote somewhere along the line. Eh, let's just call it a Savini-*ism* and keep moving on!

On Day 10 we talked about our feelings and the importance of *feeling* the feeling because you can't heal what you don't feel. Your feelings are real and important. They will guide and direct you positively if you allow them. Today, you're going to learn how to trust your gut and understand the difference between inner wisdom and fear. Trust is an important factor in your quest to love yourself and be your own hero. You need to know that you can always depend on your hero, don't you?

When I Listen to the Voice Within, I Win

In the past decade I have come to rely on my inner sense of wisdom more and more. Whenever I make decisions – large or small – I go by how it *feels* to me. I'm not talking about the feelings we discussed on Day 10 (sadness, happiness, joy, disappointment, etc.). Instead, I'm talking about what it feels like in your heart, your body, and your soul (a.k.a. the gut feeling). Notice, I did not say in your mind. The mind gets in our way when we are making decisions. In general, when you come to a point of deciding, there is something deep within you that is leaning towards one thing or another. If you would just go with that feeling, you'd be a happy person. Unfortunately, we generally allow the mind to chime in with an opinion, and this is where fear takes over. That feeling you got when you first contemplated a decision or idea is the voice of love. It *is* your inner wisdom. Your inner wisdom comes from your soul, body, and heart working together. It is also known as your gut feeling. Hence, the term 'go with your gut.' That pit you feel in the bottom of your stomach is the voice of fear rising from your mind. You see, your heart is really the one in charge. The heart truly *knows* everything, but the mind *thinks* it knows everything. Your mind has way too much ego and thrives on being right. Your heart is humble and just lets the mind think what it wants. Often, people say, 'trust your gut.' Well, your gut is the feeling that you get from your soul, body, and heart connecting. Here's what happens; you get an idea about a person, place, or thing, your soul gives you a feeling that passes through your heart, and then sends a message throughout your body. It's not really your physical gut that is involved here, but moreover, a feeling you get throughout your body that lets you know the right path for you. If you would listen at that point and move forward, then all would be well. Instead, 9 out of 10 times, the mind chimes in with *what if's* and all hell breaks loose! I'm not sure I'm conveying this 'science' lesson well. Let me give you an example;

You are driving down the street and something deep inside you tells you to take a detour. Your mind chimes in and says, 'Detour? Why would you take a detour?

Stay the course. There's no reason to change our plan. We might be late if you do. Don't do it. You're being crazy.' You listen to the voice of fear and decide not to take the detour only to end up in traffic for over an hour because there was an accident up ahead that you couldn't have foreseen! Now, if you just listened to the voice within and trusted yourself, you would have avoided the long wait.

Here's another example;

You meet someone and your initial reaction to their energy is an uneasy feeling. You're not sure what it is, but they just rub you the wrong way. Your mind chimes in again and tells you that you are over-reacting or being judgmental. You start to go back and forth between the head and the heart. You choose to ignore the red flags that are popping up with this person. Several months later you are in a toxic relationship with them and digging your way out of an emotional ditch!

I make most decisions in my life based upon how it *feels* in my heart, body, and soul. Even when I choose a book in the store. I walk down the aisles, pick up a book, touch the cover and finger through the pages to feel the energy. I then do the same with other books and when I find one that *feels* right to me, I head to the counter to pay for it. I might be a little bit extreme, but I can tell you one thing for sure, when my head gets in the way, I am full of anxiety and indecision. When I center myself and go with what *feels* right, I am peaceful, joyful, and confident. The answers *are* within.

You Are an Energetic Being

You, me, the guy next door, the people on TV and around the world are all made of energy. We are energetic beings having a human experience. We may not always be aware of it, but we are emitting signals at all points in our day due to the energy in our whole being. Think of animals or small children. Babies read other people's energy without effort. Have you ever noticed what happens when a baby is picked up by an individual that doesn't feel right to them? They tense up, cry, and wiggle their away from them. Animals have this innate ability as well. They greet some humans with glee or back away and become frantic with others. They are sensing a person's energy and not questioning it with their mind. When we think negative thoughts, our energy is uncomfortable and somewhat agitated. This is when you feel anxious, as if you are jumping out of your skin. Some might call this out of balance. When we are centered in our mind, body, and spirit, our energy is peaceful and calm. I have known this to be true even when there are awful events occurring around me. If I am centered in that moment, then I know all is well and I am on the right path. If I allow my mind to chime in with doubt and fear, then everything falls apart; I can't think straight, question everything, have difficulty making decisions, and feel completely lost.

The exercises in this book will most definitely help you to center yourself and balance your energy. Once you can do that, you will be able to hear the voice of love louder than the voice of fear and you will finally trust yourself. Sometimes, we are fooled because when a thought comes to our mind, we believe that's our gut or intuition giving us a sign. However, if you have frantic, uneasy energy in your body, then this is not the voice of love. Instead, it is your mind chiming in with the voice of fear. In today's exercise, you will learn how to relax your body and ease the mind to get to that *gut feeling*. We're going to get the mind out of the way so the soul, heart and body can navigate you through your life effectively and positively. You ready?

Today's Exercise:

4) Think of one situation where you are trying to decide something. It can be about a person, an event, an idea, etc.

   Ex) Is this the right house for me to buy for my family?

5) Sit back comfortably and close your eyes.

6) Put your hands on your heart and ask your question (s) simply.

7) Ex) What does it feel like to stay in my current home? What would it feel like in the new home?

8) Pay attention to your body's response when you ask. If you feel frantic, uneasy or nervous, then that is the voice of fear. It is not your soul, heart and body working together. If you feel peaceful, uplifted, joyful or at ease, then that is the voice of love guiding you towards this choice.

9) Then, trust yourself. Trust that your inner guidance has spoken and do NOT allow the mind to chime in with fear. The moment the doubts and questions begin to flood your mind, stop the thoughts, breathe deeply and re-center yourself. At this point you may want to choose your mindfulness tool to go back to your breath and re-center. You may also want to say a few affirmations to turn the thoughts around while asking yourself if this is serving you or sabotaging you.

Practice this throughout the day with small decisions; what you'd like to eat, what clothes to wear, where to sit at a seminar, etc. Keep practicing this throughout the remainder of the 30-day commitment and into your life afterwards and you will be a much happier person. This, I guarantee!

Now, go have a great day with one thing in mind; trust yourself because the answers *are* within.

You've got this!

Lots of Love & Tons of Light,

Vicki

Journal Entry: Tonight, write about your experiences throughout your day. Discuss the feelings in your body and how you can determine the difference between love and fear.

*If you are signed up for the membership, there is a great video to further describe this concept of learning to listen to the gut (your soul, heart, and body working together). www.vickisavini.com/member

Day 24: Detox from Distraction

"When there is no distraction, there is clarity."
~Lorii Myers

We live in a crazy, busy, and hectic society. Most of us walk around sporting a tiny (or not so tiny) computer in our hands that we call a phone. We fool ourselves into thinking we are connected to one another because within moments we can send messages, retrieve documents, or transport a photo or video across the globe. Yet, is this true? Are we truly connected because we have social media and instant accessibility to people? Not so much.

Let's be honest with one another here, social media is a lie and we spend way too much time on electronics. We scroll through 'Fakebook' looking at the lives of others and convince ourselves that *they* have everything we believe we lack. We look at pictures on Instagram and immediately assume a fantasy story behind the pictures we view. Research reveals that addiction to social media is *real* in our society. Not only is it addictive but it has proven to be depressive. Why is that? It's addictive because it gives us immediacy, and depressive because we get a sense of self-worth from it. These hand-held devices – we can't leave home without – have given us a new way to search for approval outside of ourselves. We easily get drawn in and have become conditioned to search for instant gratification. You know what happens. You post a picture and then can't help but check back to see who liked or commented on your picture. Am I enough? Am I worthy? Am I important, lovable, or safe? You see where this is going. We are validating that core belief by scrolling through social media and seeking approval. Aside from that, we beat up on ourselves as we create false stories about the lives of others and demean our own. It's not like we even set out to do this on purpose. It's totally subconscious. When you see a person's true colors, you can never see them the way you did previously. It's the same with this addiction to social media, once you see how it distracts you and controls your life, you can never ignore that again.

Having this attachment to our mini computers goes deeper than social media. Since we have the capability of this false connection at our fingertips, we run the risk of overworking, overthinking, and overanalyzing. What's more important is we are *not* truthfully connecting with others. Sadly, we are completely disconnected from the people who are in our physical presence. When a notification pops up on the phone you may find it difficult to ignore. It is hard to be present in the moment because when the phone vibrates or dings, you have been trained like Pavlov's dog to react in some way. Albert Einstein once said, "I fear the day that technology will surpass our human interaction. The world will have a generation of idiots." Ouch! Are we approaching that horizon? Now, you *are* aware, and you know after our journey together this far that awareness is the first step to healing. We have somehow become a slave to our hand-held devices and it's something we need to explore deeper as we learn to love ourselves. So, today, let's detox from this distraction – even for just a tiny bit of time.

What's the Big Deal?

Distractions. We are distracted from our own hopes, dreams, and lives by overindulging in social media and electronics in general. It takes your time, energy, and attention away from those you love. Watch a group of teens sit together at an event. They all have their phones in their hands. They barely look at one another, yet their heads are buried in their phones as they text, tweet, snapchat, or post photos on Instagram.

Sure, you might see them occasionally interact to get a selfie here and there with their friends, but for the most part, they are staring at an electronic device. Now, look a little deeper into the crowd. Look at the adults around them. They too are often engrossed in their phones. If it's not social media, it's emails or texting, especially if you are a single parent and looking for love through online dating. I won't get that conversation started here because that literally *is* an entirely different book! The point is, we are all distracted from the current moment. We are not in the here and now, enjoying the time we have with one another. Instead, we are searching for approval outside of ourselves. By spending most of our time on our hand-held computers, we are watching life happen instead of living our lives. It's easy to allow yourself to be distracted with social media. Years ago, we didn't have this luxury and we were forced to have face-to-face conversations and physical interaction. Don't get me wrong, technology is a beautiful thing, yet in moderation. If I am being honest, the hand-held device has taken over my life as well. When I get to a point where I feel that I am constantly checking my phone, I know I need to step back and ask what it is I'm searching for or avoiding. That's why we engross ourselves in social media and busy ourselves with checking emails and apps. We are looking to escape our current situation or perhaps our life at that moment. I have learned that spending too much time focused on social media and the phone in general is not a good way to love myself. I need all the energy I can get to build myself up and stay the course of taking care of me first. I'm gathering you will as well. Is it possible that your hand-held device has become a distraction for you? Might you spend too much time 'checking out' on social media? And, do you honestly feel good when you're spending this much time on devices? If you can walk away from your phone easily and the vibration or ding doesn't make your heart jump as you seek approval outside of yourself, then go ahead and skip today's exercise. However, if any of the above makes sense to you and you feel that social media is overtaking your life, or at least taking up too much time, then let's detox.

Today's Exercise:

1) Ask yourself which *media* is taking away most of your time and energy. Is it Facebook, Instagram, Snapchat, emails, texting, or other apps.

2) Start your day by writing a message to your friends on your media of choice. Tell them today, you are taking a break from social media to focus on life that's happening right in front of you. Or, make a choice to just walk away for the day and not give an explanation. Truthfully, you don't need to explain your absence.

3) When you start your day (after your morning daily practice 😊), place the phone in a conspicuous place and turn off notifications. Our brains have been subconsciously programmed to react to the notifications that come up on our phone. Give yourself some space. Do *not* allow yourself to check the phone constantly. Put the ringer on silent and decide to only check your phone as needed depending on your family and work needs. Perhaps it's every hour at the top of the hour or at lunch and then dinner time. Try to forget about this device (it may be difficult). If you are out with your kids, spouse, a friend, etc. do NOT take the phone out. Leave it where it is. I understand if you have children and need to be available to them, but you don't need to check it all the time. ***No social media today***. No

Facebook, Instagram, Snapchat, etc. None, nada. The only excuse you might have to go on social media today is if you own a business and you post daily. Then, go ahead and preload your posts for the day in the early morning and do *not* go back to check until later in the evening after dinner.

4) Make it a point to be present in the moment with all interactions today and refrain from grabbing that phone.

I know this exercise may be one of the most difficult tasks yet but go with it and see how you feel at the end of the day. It's one day; not a week, not a month, not a year – just a day. Detox and then you can add it back in with moderation.

Now, go have a great day with one thing in mind; detox from distraction. Take this day (and possibly more) to detox from the social media and mini computer distraction.

You've got this!

Lots of Love & Tons of Light,

Vicki

Journal Entry: Tonight, write about your experiences throughout your day. Discuss how you felt without your hand-held device attached to you. Write how social media has affected your life in the past 6 months and what you'd like to do to change that.

Day 25: Get Connected

*"I define connection as the energy between
people when they feel seen, heard, and
valued; when they can give and receive
without judgement; and when they
derive sustenance and strength from the
relationship."*
~Brene Brown

We all crave it. There's no denying it. Not one person in this world wants to be completely alone all the time. There is a huge difference between being alone and loneliness. Loneliness is the sense that you are alone in the world. It is the feeling that you are not seen, heard, or valued. Being alone is a choice. Sometimes, we choose to spend time alone to balance ourselves, be creative, or go within. Ultimately though, we all long for human connection – and not only surface level connection, but deep, intimate connection. This kind of connection fuels us. We learn about ourselves, others, and the world around us by the deep connections we share with others.

At my darkest hour, I felt lonely. It was one of the most awful feelings a human being can be exposed to. I didn't have the love that I *thought* I had. My son was at an age where he was off playing with his friends or on his Xbox. He wasn't interested in hanging with mom who was depressed as hell. I ended up spending a great deal of time alone in my home – not by choice, but because my son was playing in the neighborhood, I wouldn't just hop in my car and go off. People would tell me I needed to get out, but I wasn't sure how the hell to do that because I have my son 90% of the time and he was off doing his own thing. That left social media, my backyard, the dogs, and online dating to take the loneliness away. None of those worked very well, although the dogs always made me feel loved. I cried a lot of tears with them. They absorbed my tears in their soft fur and often licked my face dry. Thank God for our furry friends. When I would go out with friends, I was so miserable that I'm quite sure I was tough to be around. People know me as a ray of sunshine and there was no sunshine during this dark period. I often felt like an observer of my own life. It felt as if I was staring at my life like a Lifetime movie, and the movie continued with no commercial breaks. I believed at the deepest level that I was not important. I most definitely felt that I wasn't seen, heard, or valued. That, of course, was a lie. I was simply focused on the wrong kind of attention. I was seeking the love of a man who was incapable of truly loving another human being, and that was prompting me to feel empty on so many levels. I also did not love myself and would therefore take crumbs of affection or false friendship to ease the loneliness. It took months afterwards for me to come to the deep understanding that I was never truly alone. I learned that I wasn't alone because I had my higher power, and myself. As I learned to love myself, there were still times when I felt lonely, so I learned to develop skills to ease and finally release that feeling. The skills I developed are some of the best exercises in this book, because what eased the pain the most, was truly loving the girl staring back at me in the mirror.

Ease the Lonely

I have come to realize that there are many people out there who feel lonely. It doesn't matter if you are married, single, in a partnership, living with a full family, or all by yourself. Loneliness has nothing to do with how many people are surrounding you. Instead, it has to do with whether you feel seen, heard, and valued. You know exactly what I'm talking about. I'm sure you can recount a time when there were lots of people in a room, yet you felt lonely. Perhaps, you can remember a relationship when you slept by your partner nightly, yet you felt totally alone. There are many instances when we feel lonely. When we feel this way, it generally taps our toxic core belief because it's a way to validate that we are not enough, not worthy, not lovable, not safe, or unimportant. When you are seen, heard, and valued, you don't feel lonely. I am a firm believer, due to my experiences, that you need to be your own best friend and love yourself unconditionally to not only ease but also release the loneliness. However, you can't truly learn to love yourself without human connection. When we talk with others, listen to others, share stories with others and engage with others, we not only learn about them, but we learn about ourselves. They become a mirror for us. Sometimes, they are a clear reflection of who we are. Other times, they reflect our fears. Many times, they remind us who we truly are at the core whether they are challenging us or complimenting us. Without human connection, we cannot grow, nor will we learn to truly love ourselves for the bad, the good, and the different. If you want to ease the lonely, you must first connect with yourself. You must get to know who you are at your core, as you've been doing for the past 24 days. You must also make the effort to connect with like-minded people. Ditch the surface relationships. Trade that time for meaningful relationships where you are challenged, loved for who you are, accepted for who you are not, and welcomed no matter what.

Step out of your comfort zone. Do what makes your heart sing and find groups of people who love those same things. There are many opportunities to do this in today's society. Here is an opportunity to use social media to your advantage. Go on Facebook and look up groups that you may be interested in. Join those groups and share your time and story. Attend a workshop or seminar on something that you are interested in. Meetup is a great app to find groups of interest where you can connect with like-minded people. These are the places where you will ease the lonely because you will feel seen, heard, and valued. Understand that you are not the only person feeling lonely. You've been down many roads and you have a lot of wisdom to impart on others, just like they have for you. The roads that we take, the falls we make, the power we gain from climbing uphill all come in handy to not only help ourselves, but to inspire, empower, and encourage others. You are a rescuer. You like to help others. This is a chance to do just that in a healthy manner because you are not allowing others to overstep your boundaries any longer. Wipe the tears of loneliness away and get out there and share your story, share your thoughts, and share your love. What you've been through just might help others. What you're going through, someone else has already conquered and they may be able to guide you. Connect with people who are like-minded. Then, you will feel seen, heard, and valued.

Today's Exercise:

1) Today, you will step out of your comfort zone. Look up groups or activities that you are interested in. Make a plan to go to a new group or activity and experience something that makes your heart sing. If you can go to a group today, then have at it. If the group isn't meeting today but you made the effort to look it up and sign up, give yourself a gold star.

2) List three people you feel you have deep connections with. These are the people you feel seen, heard, and valued with.

   a) _____
   _____

   b) _____
   _____

   c) _____
   _____

Do you see at least one of these people weekly? If not, make a commitment to do so. If you don't have three, make the effort to find another friend who you can feel seen, heard and be valued by.

3) If you should feel lonely today and there isn't a group, an activity with like-minded people or someone you feel seen, heard, and valued with, then be your own best friend. Take the time to

remind yourself how far you've come and go do something from the previous 24 days that nourishes your soul. Be there for yourself. Remind yourself that you've got this.

Now, go have a great day with one thing in mind; connect with like-minded people.

You've got this!

Lots of Love & Tons of Light,

Vicki

Journal Entry: What makes you feel lonely? When was the last time you felt lonely? How can you ease and release the lonely in your life?

*There is a video on easing and releasing the loneliness on the membership site. www.vickisavini.com/member

Day 26: Plug In ∞

"The power within you is infinite. Plug into your higher self for a surge you thought was unattainable."

~Mary-Frances Winters

I believe it was 2011 when I began writing my first empowerment book, "Ignite the Light: Empowering Children & Adults to Be Their Absolute Best." My dad had passed in late 2009, and I was still healing from the loss. In that book, I wrote about 7 Essentials that we all need to build a strong foundation in childhood and help us to navigate the waters of life successfully in adulthood. Those 7 essentials came to me one-by-one, exactly the way the 30-day commitment in this book came (yes, I went through all 30 exercises too). The Universe has a way of getting messages through me by making me get down and dirty first, and then giving me the words to share. When I first began writing that book I knew there were going to be 7 Essentials, but I had no idea what they were! The Universe literally put me through a lesson for each essential and then the words just poured out effortlessly to create the book. I had written 6 essentials and then came to a screeching halt for months. I was feeling frustrated with the writing process and life in general. I remember going into my healing room – where I see my clients – and trying to click the light switch to turn it on. When I clicked it, the light flickered and then went out. I thought to myself, "Of course!" and then plopped on the couch with a deep feeling of defeat. That's when the tears came. I was depressed because my marriage was failing, I had writer's block, my dad (who was my rock) was gone, and I felt overwhelmed and totally drained. I laid there for close to an hour and then I heard a voice within say, "You're not plugged in." I distinctly remember being pissed and looking out at the sky and saying, "What the hell does that mean?" Within a few moments I noticed that the plug that was connected to the light (which turned the light on when you clicked the switch) was not quite in the wall outlet. I pushed the plug into the outlet and the light came on. It was obvious to me that the Universe wasn't just trying to tell me that the plug was out of the wall. That was much too simple. There was something bigger going on. Within a few moments, it hit me. I wasn't plugged in to my higher power!

You see, after my dad passed, I became somewhat angry with God. It was so sudden that I felt like I was hit by a 2x4 and I wasn't sure how to process it all. Instead of going inward and digging deeper into my spirituality, I boycotted it. I'm not a very religious person. However, I am very spiritual. I firmly believe that there is something bigger than us out there and that we are all connected energetically. I'm a person who goes by what feels right, as I've stated before. Committing myself to one church or one philosophy has never felt right to me. Instead, I love to experience all different religions from Christianity to Buddhism to hugging trees! I take what resonates with me and leave the rest behind. At that time, I wasn't connecting with Spirit at all; no meditating, no nature walks, no reading of spiritual literature, no groups, no churches, nada. This was a clear message, not only for the 7th essential in my book, but also for me in my life. I have now come to realize without plugging in to – what I like to call – Source energy, I am limiting myself, and so are you.

Your Higher Self

My first official book was a children's book. That book was titled, "The Light Inside of Me," and was published in May of 2010. In that book, I teach children we each have a light deep inside us that guides us and reminds us who we truly are. The main lesson in that book is to listen to the voice within, do what feels right, and trust yourself (as you learned on Day 23). We *are* energetic beings and when we are in alignment with our highest good, our inner light shines brightly. This is when everything flows easily and effortlessly. When we are out of alignment, our inner light is dim, and we hit every bump, road block, and wall. My light is bright when I am coaching clients, running workshops, writing books (like the one you are reading now), teaching my 1st graders, and watching my son turn into an amazing young man. I know that I've done something great with each of these things. I'm clear with each that I am serving my purpose. When I am teaching, writing, or speaking, I am aligned with my higher self. It's a rush of powerful energy that cannot be explained in words but needs to be experienced. You become more in touch with your inner light by plugging in to Source energy. For me, that's meditating, reading, writing, and engaging in the beauty of life. For some, attending a church service or spiritual lecture ignites the inner light. For others, being artistic or communing with nature connects them to the light. We all have something that ignites our spirit. That one thing (or a few) that makes you feel alive inside and gives you a joy that nothing else can. When you are out of alignment, you feel it in your energy. When I was dating Richard, I was dim most of the time. I literally felt as though I couldn't think straight. I was a shell of the woman I am meant to be in this life and the person I am today. When we are desperately trying to rescue someone else, we are dim; our energy gets drained and we are distracted from who we truly are. It is imperative that we learn to connect to Source energy to ignite the light within and truly be our best selves.

Connecting to Source Energy

Source energy is always available. It is just like that outlet in the wall in my healing room. The energy is always available to bring the light or ignite the spirit. However, it is up to you to plug into it. On the first day of school when my son started kindergarten, I arrived home from a long day to be graced with his deep and profound wisdom. The first day of school is always exhausting for teachers, especially in elementary school. I walked into our home through the garage and into the mudroom with bags weighing me down on each arm. My bright 5-year-old bounced into the small space cornering me at the door and said, "Hi Mom! What's God?" I hadn't exposed him to church, per se, but we always read spiritual children's book such as, "The Little Soul and the Sun," by Neal Donald Walsh. There was no formal religious education happening in our home because of my own beliefs. Plus, Nico always had a way of spitting out profound messages in the most surprising moments and I didn't want to taint that. It was too pure to disrupt. I was stunned when he asked such a big question though. I put my bags down gently and kneeled to give him a hug and then I said, "What makes you ask? Did you hear something at school about God?" He replied, "Nope! It's just what my brain is asking." I then looked at him, took a deep breath, and said, "Well, buddy, what do *you* think?" He put his finger on his chin, looked up at the ceiling, paused for a few moments, then his eyes lit up and he confidently said, "Oh! I know! It's the Energy of the Light!" I stood there in awe wondering what just happened, and then I smiled to myself. My little avatar had schooled me once again – on the first day of his kindergarten experience!

That little five-year-old had more knowledge than I could've ever imagined. In my humble opinion and experience, he was absolutely correct about God. A few years later, when the above 'light situation' occurred, I remember reminiscing about that very day and smiling once again as I thought to myself, "I really should've listen to my kid back then!"

So, what is Source energy? Source energy is God. It is Universal light. It is the chi that flows through us and illuminates our planet. It is 'something bigger' that is out there that we all need to plug into to *be* our absolute best. Your higher power might be called God, Jesus, Buddha, Goddess, Spirit, or the Energy of the Light. It doesn't matter what you call it. What matters is that you plug into something bigger. Plugging in will give you the strength and wisdom that you need to stay in touch with that light within. It will help you to remember you are never alone and you are *always* supported. It is, quite honestly, your life force in so many ways, whether you believe it to be a being, nature, or an energy. It's always available, but we must plug in to reap the rewards.

How do you connect to the *energy of the light*? Meditate, pray, attend church or a spiritual group, read, reflect, dance, sing, paint, play music, walk in nature, etc. Connect to your inner light. This is another way for you to love yourself and it will give you a strength that you cannot receive from anything else.

Today's Exercise:

1) How do you connect to Spirit?

_____

_____

_____

_____

_____

_____

2) What one small task can you complete daily to connect to your inner light?

_____

_____

_____

_____

_____

_____

Ex) Say a prayer, meditate, or read a spiritual passage daily.

3) Connect with Source Energy today by saying out loud, "I am willing." Say this, three times as often as you can throughout the day. I have found that when I speak these words, great spiritual lessons come forward and remind me that I am always supported by the Universe.

Now, go have a great day with one thing in mind; connect to the light inside to feel the power that is deep within you.

You've got this!

Lots of Love & Tons of Light,

Vicki

Journal Entry: Discuss how you feel when you are connected to Source Energy. Then discuss how you feel when you are disconnected. How can you welcome Source Energy into your life more frequently?

*If you are a member on the member site come meet my son Nico to gather some of his wisdom.

www.vickisavini.com/member

Day 27: Your Loooooooove Language

*"All of us blossom when we feel loved and
wither when we do not feel loved."*
~Gary Chapman

Several years ago, while trying to find some way to
connect with my husband, I picked up a powerful book
titled, "The Five Love Languages," by Gary Chapman.
I had hoped we would read the book together and
discover how to connect and love one another. That
didn't work out so well, but I *did* learn a great deal
about myself in reading that book. I learned my love
language – the way in which I *feel* love. We all want
to feel loved, but we speak different languages of
love. This book explained to me how I received love
and how my ex-husband received love as well. It was
eye opening to see why we were so distant from one
another. I loved this book so much that when Gary
Chapman wrote another book titled, "The Five Love
Languages for Children," I devoured that book in a few
hours on a beach one summer and learned not only

how my son best receives love, but how many of my students receive love as well! This has helped me to be a better mom and teacher.

When I went on this beautiful journey of learning to love myself, this book popped into my mind again. To truly feel loved, you need someone to speak your language. Whether you have a significant other in your life or not, you receive and show love in a certain language. It appeared to me that since there was no significant other in my life, it was important for me to not only understand my love language, but give myself the love I truly needed, wanted, and desired. This chapter will be short and sweet. I will give you the gist of the Love Languages and an exercise to empower you to love yourself in the best way for you. However, I do encourage you to pick up, "The Five Love Languages," to dig deeper. Let's dig in a bit now!

According to Gary Chapman there are five love languages; Words of Affirmation, Acts of Service, Receiving Gifts, Quality Time, and Physical Touch. These love languages are how we receive love. In other words, the way in which we most feel loved.

Words of Affirmation: are words of encouragement, praise and appreciation.

A person whose love language is *Words of Affirmation* loves to be affirmed. They can never hear the words 'I love you' enough and they so appreciate compliments and encouraging words.

Acts of Service: doing something kind to show love.

A person whose love language is *Acts of Service* feels completely loved and adored by the actions behind the words. These people are firm believers that actions speak louder than words and greatly appreciate people who initiate efforts of service to make their lives easier.

Receiving Gifts: receiving gifts as a token of love and appreciation.

A person whose love language is *Receiving Gifts* feels most loved when they are surprised with gifts. It doesn't necessarily have to be material gifts, but love-notes or small tokens of appreciation suffice as well.

Quality Time: giving undivided attention.

A person whose love language is *Quality Time* looks forward to uninterrupted time and feels most love when they have your undivided attention.

Physical Touch: physical touch makes this person feel loved.

A person whose love language is *Physical Touch* needs to be touched to feel loved. A gentle touch, a back rub, or a hug go a long way.

When I read the book years ago, I learned that *Words of Affirmation* is my #1 love language. There's nothing I appreciate more, than to be affirmed with kind words. I thrive on hearing kind and encouraging words and negative words or insults can literally shatter me. Hearing the words 'I love you' always makes my heart smile and a look of appreciation sends tingles down my spine. Knowing that my language is Words of Affirmation has helped me to understand how to *love myself* in the best way possible. You see, what this says to me is that when that voice of fear gets loud, I need to find an immediate way to silence it because if I allow the voice to grow louder, then it could shatter me. Since I love myself so very much now, I no longer allow that voice to increase in volume and destroy my sense of self-worth and esteem. I also learned that I need to hear kind, loving, and encouraging words. Therefore, mirror work isn't only good for me, it's essential to my well-being! I not only do mirror work in the morning, but as often as possible. I also set reminders on my phone to tell me the words I might need to hear to give myself a little boost throughout the day. My second highest language is *Acts of Service*. This makes me give a conscious effort to putting myself first and doing what serves me in every moment of my day. I am constantly asking myself if this is serving or sabotaging me. When I feel a bit blue, I stop and ask myself what it is that I need. I give myself the words of encouragement by using affirmations or tapping and then I do something kind for myself. That might mean taking a hot, aromatherapy shower or bath, going to get a massage, putting cozy clothes on and snuggling with my boys, or taking some time for just me. Knowing your love language will not only help if you are in a partnership, but you will be able to love yourself more completely!

Today's Exercise:

Right now, go to www.5lovelanguages.com and click the box that says, "Learn Your Love Language."

Take a few minutes to complete the quiz. Find your love language and write it here:

_____

_____

If you have two that are very close numerically, then write both.

Now, either scroll through the site or use the above information to list ways that you can love yourself more completely.

Examples:

➤ If your love language is *Words of Affirmation*, you need to find ways to praise yourself and hear kind words of appreciation. You read what I do above.

➤ If your love language is *Acts of Service*, you need to be proactive to think ahead and find ways to make your life easier. I will also say that doing random acts of service for others will also make you feel loved if this is your love language.

➤ If your love language is Receiving Gifts, you might want to give yourself the gift of time, chocolate, a pampering session etc. Go ahead and gift yourself. There's nothing wrong with that!

➤ If your love language is *Quality Time,* you need to find ways to give yourself the time that you need, want, and desire. Plan out time with friends, your partner, your kids, or me time.

➤ If your love language is *Physical Touch,* go get a massage, give a hug, ask for a hug, or snuggle with your kids or pets.

Be creative! You can totally have fun with this.

Now, go have a great day with one thing in mind; love yourself by speaking your own love language.

You've got this!

Lots of Love & Tons of Light,

Vicki

Journal Entry: How did it feel to actively love yourself today according to your love language? What can you do daily to give yourself the love that you need? What are some other ways that you can love yourself according to your #1 love language?

Day 28: Your Body is Your Temple ∞

"Your body is your temple. Keep it pure and clean for the soul to reside in."
~B.K.S Iyengar

You only get one body in this life. This is your vehicle from the moment you are born until the moment you leave this earth. It is therefore best to take care of it, love it, and cherish it as if it is the most precious gift you have. But, let's be real, you're a rescuer and you don't always put yourself first. Well, maybe you haven't in the past, but the last 27 days may have proved different for you. I'm not going to tell you what to eat or how to eat. I'm not going to tell you the best exercise plan for you. Nor, am I going to preach about organic v. non-organic. Instead, this chapter is all about looking at yourself and deciding what is right for *you*. This is a judgment-free zone, so please be real with yourself as you look in the mirror and decide how to best take care of your most precious gift. If you truly want to love yourself, you must love the skin you're in. You can't do that unless you accept yourself for who you are. You won't do that, unless you've done a conscious inventory of what you like about your body, what you'd like to change, and what is best for your body.

What You Put in Your Body

Food

For several years I was a pescatarian. That is a vegetarian who also eats fish. I had decided that meat was no longer for me. I didn't like the texture, the thought of animals dying for me, or how my body felt after eating meat. I thought I was doing the right thing for my body, however the Universe showed me the opposite. After several years of living this way and putting what I thought was healthy food into my body (legumes, whole oats, raw vegetables, etc.), I was diagnosed with *Leaky Gut Syndrome.* I had to go through a complete detox and change my eating habits. I was feeling weak, bloated, and lethargic most of the time. I also had other strange 'leaky' issues that most doctors could not explain. Thank God I found a functional medical doctor who knew his shit. He was able to help me understand that not all bodies are alike. He also taught me how to understand what *my* body needed. I now know I need to limit certain foods for my body to be at optimal health. I'm not saying that being a pescatarian or vegetarian is bad. I'm simply stating that it's not right for all body types. You need to listen to your body just as you learned to listen to your gut on Day 23. When I eat food, I am now conscious of what is happening within my body. I have come to know that white flour, gluten, and legumes can bloat me unless I eat them in moderation. Peppers are not good for my body, as much as I love them, and milk products build a great deal of phlegm for me, causing issues with congestion and headaches. I don't totally have to avoid these foods, but I only ingest them in moderation. I'm not a huge junk food junky (unless it's that time of the month when I crave salt and sweets). I don't like the way my body feels when I eat junk. If you put junk into your body, you're going to feel junky, plain and simple. As for alcohol. Well, I'm 5'1" and I weigh about 115 pounds. I therefore do not tolerate many drinks before getting 'stupid' so I generally don't drink much. I also don't like the way my body feels if I have more than three drinks. I don't like to be out of control, have no need to numb my feelings or urinate several times in an hour, and I can do without feeling like shit the next day. Therefore, alcohol is not an issue for me and my body thanks me for this. Drugs. I've never been one to tolerate medication well. I don't even like to take Advil for my headache! Recreational drugs have never appealed to me because, like I said, I like to be in control of myself and own my power. I'm happy to be the designated driver because I enjoy living. With that said, I have friends who engage in these activities. I don't judge them. I'm always there to make sure they get home safely, but that's not what I would put in my body because I firmly believe that my body is *my* temple.

Exercise

This is the one that I am horrible at. When I was in my early 20's, I was in the gym 5-6 days a week because I competed in the Miss America System for seven years. It was obviously important to me to be in very good shape because I was periodically walking across a stage in front of thousands of people in my swimsuit! Once I was in the habit, I did just fine. However, I've never been one to love working out. I am a very active person, though. I am constantly on the go with my son and two dogs. I have a few flights of stairs in my home that I am up and down several times a day. I do enjoy going to yoga at least once a week and when I feel lethargic or low on energy, I kick myself in the ass and get back to an exercise regimen, even if it's 3x's a week. This would be the area that I would most certainly work on for myself because I could be taking better care of my body in this regard. We should not only exercise to look good, but rather to keep the body at optimal health, especially as we begin to age (ugh, and I thought I was a forever teenager).

Mental Health

Your mental health can greatly improve of decrease your body functioning, as you well know. The more stress you allow in your life, the more damage you do to your physical vessel. Just look at the headlines and you will see that stress and mental imbalance are causing havoc throughout the world. Allowing too much stress in your life will most definitely deplete the body's ability to function optimally. Not getting enough sleep, ingesting high amounts of caffeine to sustain a tight schedule, overworking, not relaxing, and putting stress on the heart and body by worrying too much, is not taking care of your body. It is critical to use the tools in this book to lower your stress and increase a positive outlook if you'd like to have optimal health. I've spent a great deal of time throughout this book on your mental well-being so I'm not going to overstate the obvious here; set your intentions, affirm positive thoughts, honor your boundaries, don't take everything personally, be in the moment, remember the 80:20 rule, and take care of you. 'Nuff said. Everything starts in the mind as discussed earlier in this book. Sometimes, we just need to shift the perspective a bit and suddenly our whole world looks completely different.

Today's Exercise:

Go out and run three miles! No, just joking. Come on, you know me better than that.

Remember your main goal is to love the skin you're in. When you look in the mirror, you must love that person staring back at you before anyone else can. If you see something you don't like (you personally, not someone else), then create a plan and work to change that. There are some things you need to learn to accept and love just the way you are, but I have confidence that you can determine these factors at this point. Today you will begin with a conscious inventory pertaining to your body. Take your time and be honest. I will first define each section and then you will fill out a worksheet. If you are a member on the site, there's a nifty PDF (www.vickisavini.com/member). If not, you can fill it in right here in the book.

Conscious Inventory for My Body
Date: _____

1) ***What I like about my body or what I feel grateful for***. Determine what it is that you currently like about your body. Take a step back and honor your wins. Examples; I like that I have a small frame, my body has been good to me so far, I have thick healthy hair.

2) ***What I'd like to change about my body.*** Think about each of the categories I wrote about above. Is there something you'd like to change about your diet, alcohol consumption, etc. When you look in the mirror is there an aspect of your body you'd like to change? Be cautious to look at your own body and only change what *you* do not like. Do not change your body – in any way – to appease someone else. That is *not* loving yourself.

3) ***What is best for my body?*** Look at both columns you've filled out and then determine your best course of action. Determine what you will need to help your body feel better. Is it exercise, a different diet or perhaps less stress? Examples; It is best for me to eat healthier. It is best for me to exercise more often. I need to lay off the wine at night. When you complete the chart, you will move on to one health goal you'd like to focus on first and then you can expand to extended periods of time. What is the health goal you'd like to focus on first? Remember, loving yourself means loving the vehicle you're in as well. Your body *is* your temple.

Now, go ahead and mindfully fill the chart below.

What I like about my body or what I am grateful for.	What I'd like to change about my body.	What is best for my body.

Determine one thing you'd like to do to improve the health of your body.

One thing I'd like to change in the next 10 days is

_____.

In the next 30 days I'd like to _____

_____.

A 3-month goal for me is _____

_____.

A 6-month goal for me is _____

_____.

By the time 12 months have passed I will _____

_____

_____.___

_____

Now, go have a great day with one thing in mind; your body *is* your temple.

You've got this!

Lots of Love & Tons of Light,

Vicki

Journal Entry: What are some ways that you've abused your body in your lifetime? How are you going to commit to taking better care of your body? If you made any changes today for your body, write about how that felt.

Day 29: A Whole New World ∞

"If you change the way you look at things,
the things you look at change."
~Dr. Wayne Dyer

Is the glass half full, or half empty? Is the voice of love, or the voice of fear what you hear most? Is everything happening to you, or might it just be happening *for* you? Perspective is everything. The way in which we look at life can make a huge impact on our happiness. I don't know about you, but I like being a happy girl! Sure, I've had my share of bumps in the road and near-death experiences, but all-in-all, I'm thankful for everything that has happened. Without this path that I've taken, I would not be who I am today. And I really like who I am today. As a matter of fact, I love myself!

I've always been the kind of person who tries to see the good in everything. Remember at the onset of this book when I told you that I could see the best in the worst human being? Yeah, well, there is an upside to that...

I've had so many people tell me, 'I am so very sorry that you had to go through a divorce' or worse yet 'I'm sorry you had the experience of Dick.' When I hear people say those words to me I always smile and say, "I'm not!" They generally tilt their heads and look at me with a funny look of confusion on their face. I then tell them that I'm grateful that I had those experiences because I learned the most from the most awful experiences in my life. Divorce sucks – yeah it does – but I learned that I got married for the wrong reasons. I wasn't ready to get married. I hadn't done my healing work on myself. Of course, that relationship was never going to work. The blessing is my son, Nico. He is the light of my life. I don't know who I would be without being his mom. Being his mom completes a part of me that nothing else in my life can ever fill. My rocky road with Richard was heart-wrenching, yes, but I don't believe I would've found my power without that experience. I know I wouldn't love myself the way I do now, and you wouldn't be holding this book in your hands (or reading it on a device) at this very moment. Again, I am grateful. I'm not grateful for him being a crappy human being, but I am grateful for the lesson. Sometimes, your heart must break a million times before it can truly break open. That's what happened for me. I continually chose toxic, unhealthy relationships until I hit my absolute rock bottom. It was then, and only then, that I realized I needed to first love myself, thus I would never betray myself again. Perspective *is* everything. The way you look at things truly makes a huge difference. You can choose to see the glass half full, or half empty. You can choose to listen to the voice of fear over the voice of love. You can choose to believe that everything is happening to you, but when you start believing everything happens *for* you, that's when the magic happens.

Everything Happens for You

Instead of believing everything happens to you, turn that around and start to see that everything happens for you. Honestly, look back at your life, would you be where you are today without the experiences leading you here to this very moment? Bad things are going to happen. Mean people are going to come into your life. Instead of thinking, 'Why me?' turn it around and ask, 'What am I learning from this?' Or, 'What is the blessing in this lesson?' Trust that the Universe has your back and everything that is happening *is* happening for your highest good.

Can't/Won't

These are two very small words that have a massive impact on our lives. Say this sentence out loud, "*I can't do that.*" What does that feel like inside your body when you say that sentence? If you're unsure, say it again looking for the *feeling* that you get when you say those words. Do you feel like a victim? Do you feel limited or broken? Of course you do! Saying the word 'can't' is an affirmation and a belief that you can *not* do something. That *never* feels good! It is another way of saying you are unable, and that's crippling. Now say this sentence, "*I won't do that.*" What does that sentence feel like when you say it out loud? Do you feel strong, empowered and confident? Yes! This is a choice. You are saying I *will* not do that. You own the power there and you've made the conscious decision. Think of how many times you have used that word can't in your lifetime. "I'm really sorry, but I can't help out with the PTA function," "I wish I could be that person for you, but I just can't." Ouch! It hurts so bad to say the word. It's just another way of validating that core belief; I'm not enough, not worthy, not important, not safe, or not lovable. From now on, promise yourself that you are going to be mindful of these two words and the moment the 'can't' word comes to mind, bite your tongue, zip your lips, and breathe it out. Then, choose to say I won't instead. It's a whole different perspective but it's one where you own your power instead of feeling broken. Watch what happens *for* you once you make this simple little change!

Lose the Expectations

Years ago, I was reading, "The Power of Intention," by Dr. Wayne Dyer. I remember coming to one specific line in that book that struck me profoundly, *"What is meant for you will not pass you by."* At the time, I was a nervous wreck because I was about to get on the phone with the CEO of Hay House regarding my book and I was feeling pretty intimidated. I had all these high expectations of what I should say and how I should handle the conversation. I picked up Dr. Dyer's book in my office because I was trying to distract myself and chill the hell out. My son knocked on the door and asked to come in. He was four at the time. I was a little frantic because I knew Reid Tracy was going to be calling any moment. He came in and said, "I just want to give you a good luck hug mommy." He melts my heart, always. I gladly took his hug. He then pulled back and looked deep in my eyes and said, "Don't worry Mommy, it's all going to be great. Just the way it's 'spose to," then he bounced out of the room. Alas, my little avatar had spoken once again. That's when I picked up the book and opened to a random page. The first line I read was, *"What is meant for you will not pass you by."* I no sooner read the line and the phone rang. Forty-five minutes later I was agreeing to publishing my first book with Hay House.

You see, no expectation that I had would've really mattered. What was meant to be was going to be anyway. Expectations always disappoint us. We always think we have a plan, but God laughs at those plans. What happened that day, and all the days leading up to it, was *for* me. And what happened all the days leading up to today was for you too!

Today's Exercise:

Today you're going to experience something a little unconventional. What's that you say, 'the whole book has been somewhat unconventional.' Oh, yes, you're correct. Well then, today you're going to experience another fun Vicki exercise!

1) Go to a room in your home (or even your office) where there is an open corner. No furniture blocking you from standing in the corner. Yes, it's true, I'm going to ask you to stand in the corner. You remember those days, don't you? ⏎

2) Stand as close to the corner as you can, facing the corner. Your eyes should only be able to see the crease in the wall, that we like to call the corner. Close your eyes and count to ten, then open them.

3) When you open your eyes what do you see? About this time, you are asking if I've lost my mind, but stay the course. Tell me, what do you see? Right, you see a corner. There's no answer there, no opportunity, nothing of interest, correct?

4) Now, without moving from this space, turn to face the rest of the room. What do you see now? You should be seeing the furniture, windows, pets, etc.

5) Perspective is just like this. If you are looking at life like everything always happens to you, then you have your face buried in the corner, my friend. If you start looking at life like everything

happens for you, then you are open to the vast possibilities. That was fun, right?!

6) For the rest of your day, whenever the opportunity presents itself (and it will), ask yourself what the blessing is. Keep thinking about this perspective exercise and remind yourself that if it's meant for you, it will not pass you by.

Now, go have a great day with one thing in mind; everything is happening *for* you.

You've got this!

Lots of Love & Tons of Light,

Vicki

Journal Entry: Think back to a difficult time in your life. Write about how that experience helped you to grow, change or learn a very important lesson. Make sure to end your journal entry with, "Everything happens for me."

Day 30: Get Naked ∞

*"Let go of who you think you are supposed
to be and embrace who you are."*

~Brene Brown

Holy shit! Can you believe it? You've made it to Day
30. I'm so flipping proud of you. The question is, are
you proud of yourself? I sure hope so! Today you are
going to get totally naked. Don't act all shy. I told
you this was coming from the beginning of the book.
I'm naked here, and you should be too! It's all good.
You've got this by now. Today we are going to focus
on loving who you are; the bad, the good, and the
indifferent. I will lead you step-by-step. You've come a
long way. You've dug down deep, climbed mountains,
and traveled some rugged terrain. You've faced your
fears and acknowledged the love that you want, need,
and totally deserve. Now, let's turn and face the mirror
in all our nakedness!

The Bad

Okay, let's have at it. What do you suck at? What are the things you absolutely know you are awful at? I suck at bowling and billiards. I literally have no skill at either of these. To be honest, I don't really care. I also have a short fuse at times. The bowling and the billiards don't really matter in my life, so we'll talk more about them in the *indifferent* category. The short fuse, well, that's something I'm not proud of so it is something I'd like to work on. Part of getting completely naked and learning to truly love yourself is being able to see the areas of you that you aren't proud of and improving on those areas. I have a short fuse when I feel that I'm being taken advantage of or when I've said the same thing countless times to a person (like when I ask my son to pick up the dog poop and he continually ignores me). I'm Italian, but that's no excuse. I'm Sicilian. Now, that's an excuse! No, just joking. The short fuse ties into unfair expectations, taking things personally and being impatient. These are things I can work on and want to work on because they affect my personality in a way I'm not proud of. I still love myself, but I know I can use a little work in this area. There, now I am conscious. I acknowledge that I have something restricting my ability to be my best and I'd like to work on that. This is called acceptance and it feels oh so good. When we accept something about ourselves that we don't like, and we consciously decide to change, then it is easy to love yourself. You are not making excuses for yourself, but rather acknowledging something that needs work and moving forward.

Love yourself for the bad. Know that there are things that you may need to work on but that doesn't mean you're broken. It simply means you are a work in progress and since you're still living, it's good to be in progress!

The Good

What are you good at? Go ahead, don't be modest, let it shine! I am a damn good teacher. I know that even on my worst day, I am a kick-ass teacher. I can teach in my sleep. It's second nature to me. I love working with both children and adults. Kids remind me every day of the importance of loving myself. I love empowering them at such a young age and being reminded daily of the beauty of jumping, laughing, and playing. I also love teaching adults. It's an amazing feeling to watch someone light up when they see and feel their inner power. Feeling proud of yourself is healthy. You don't have to brag about it to others, but it's imperative to know what you're good at and feel the power from that.

Love yourself for the good. Know what you are good at and what you feel proud of. There's no need to hide your inner light. You were made to shine, so shine on!

The Indifferent

This is the stuff that really doesn't matter. Yeah, I'm a pretty good cook, but it doesn't matter to me. I cook to feed the fam and that's about all. Yes, I suck at bowling and billiards, but it's not that important in my life. I don't really care if you challenge me to a game of billiards and get mad because the ball goes flying off the table. It's not my thang, and I'm totes okay with that. The more comfortable you become with who you are – on every level – the more naked and fun-tastic you become (also the freer you become).

Love yourself for the indifferent. There are many things that you are good at or that you suck at that really don't matter. Don't let those things get you down. Allow them to build you up by celebrating your wins and laughing at some of the things you suck at (like billiards flying off the table).

Today's Exercise: Get Naked

Today you will look at yourself with different eyes. We will begin by making a list of the above three categories and then you will do something uncomfortable. Perhaps even more uncomfortable than getting naked!

1) What are you good at? What is something that you are really proud of? Take the time to list a few things with at least one that truly ignites that light within.

_____

_____

_____

_____

_____

_____

_____

_____

Go stand in front of a mirror and say, "I am truly proud of you for _____

_____

_____

_____

_____

_____

"

_____

2) What do you suck at? List three things you aren't so good at. Be honest with yourself and don't beat up on yourself. One of these is going to be something you are going to accept and decide to work on in some way (like me not taking things so personally or cooling my jets when I get revved up).

_Take the one that you'd like to work on or improve in your life, stand in front of the mirror and say, "Even though _____, I still deeply and completely love and accept you."_

3) Take a few things from the above list and decide which of those don't really matter. Maybe you're not a very good singer. If you're not cutting a record any time soon, does that really matter? Perhaps you aren't very good at public speaking. If you have no paid gigs coming up for public speaking, then you might consider letting that one go.

_____

_____

_____

_____

_____

_____

_____

_____

_____

_____

In front of the mirror, "It's fine that I'm not good at

_____,

I am perfectly imperfect!"

That wasn't so difficult now, was it? I think you're ready for the big kahuna!

The Uncomfortable Exercise

Choose something from your indifferent list to do in public. If you said you're a terrible singer, just start singing a song at work, on the subway, in the park, etc. Sing to the top of your lungs. Notice the stares and reactions and remind yourself that it doesn't really matter. If you are horrible at bowling, invite someone to bowl with you and just have fun totally sucking at it. If you said you're not a great cook, pick up take out and tell the family you have accepted that you're not a great cook. Enjoy! Have fun with this exercise even though it might be slightly uncomfortable. Push yourself to step out of your comfort zone and realize that at the end of this exercise you are still breathing, still alive, and the world is still spinning.

Now, go have a great day with one thing in mind; love yourself for the bad, the good, and the indifferent because you are perfectly imperfect!

Lots of Love & Tons of Light,

Vicki

Journal Entry: Take a few deep breaths and write about your day. What does it feel like to release the fear of judgment? How do you feel when you let go of the need for approval from others and you love yourself for exactly who you are?

Go Ahead, Dance Naked in the Rain

*"There's no reason to look back when you
have so much to look forward to."
~Author Unknown*

You're naked baby! You've done the work. You are aware of your deepest toxic belief. You have the tools to overcome that false belief and you now know the power that is deep within you. Light that cape on fire. You no longer need it. You don't have to hide behind a mask or pretend to be someone that you aren't. You are completely and totally free from judgment and self-doubt. Embrace this moment. Enjoy the feeling of being totally free.

You enjoy helping others. It gives you a special feeling and there's no denying that. You don't have to stop being helpful or loving. All you need to do is remember to always ask yourself, "Is this serving me or sabotaging me?" If you continue to ask yourself that question, you aren't likely to betray yourself ever again. Go out there in the world and be your best self. Be that loving, kind, gentle spirit that you are. But never, no never, allow your helping nature to leave your own well-being in the lurch. Help others, be there for them, but only with firm boundaries and *you* as the number one priority. Take the last 30 days and use the tools for the rest of your life. Don't abandon yourself. You've come too far. Continue to look in the mirror daily. Don't let a day go by without telling that person in the mirror you love them. Celebrate your wins often. Focus on the positive in life and try to remember that life isn't happening to you, it's happening *for* you. I love you and I wish you only happiness. The light in me honors the light in you.

Now, go have a great life with one thing in mind; love yourself *always* for the bad, the good, and the indifferent.

You've got this!

Lots of Love & Tons of Light,

Vicki

P.S. Now, read the next page, then get out there and dance naked in the rain!

Finally Free

For many, many years –
I've hidden behind a mask.
I showed the world only
strength and power –
In every single task.
I snapped my cape on eagerly –
To heal, to aid, to save.
Yet each time I was disappointed,
And full of utter dismay.
Beneath the mask was fear and
doubt and insecurity,
Traits I'd never show the world –
For fear of what they'd think of me.
Today, the mask is off –
And I'm ready to burn this cape.
I've learned to love myself so much –
I no longer need to escape.
I stand here totally naked –
Loving every inch of me.
It's the most amazing feeling –
For *finally,* I am free.

~Vicki Savini, *Burn the Damn Cape*

Acknowledgments

*"Gratitude makes sense of our past, brings
peace for today, and creates a vision
for tomorrow."*

~Melody Beattie

As always, I am forever grateful to my parents for raising me in the best way they knew how. I love you and appreciate everything you did throughout our lives together. I honor you for your strength, wisdom, and undying love.

I am grateful to Liz for 'turning the light on.'

I am grateful to my ex-husband, Richard, and all the other 'characters' in life's great novel who ultimately taught me to not only depend on myself but love myself no matter what.

I am grateful to Kim, Chris, Beth, Alice and the many friends who pre-read this book as I wrote and gave such poignant reviews and guidance.

A special thank you to the 'Lunch Bunch' for getting me through the 'dark period,' and being there when I needed true friends and gorgeous pictures (Sharon Beach). It's such a good thing that we have thick doors at school!

I am forever grateful to my boys; Nico, Beau, and Champ. My furry boys who always give me unconditional love, who licked my tears dry and snuggled me with love when the world felt as if it were falling apart. My beautiful, amazing son, Nico, who is always a source of inspiration and my own personal avatar. You were always so patient, kind, and supportive as I wrote this book. You are my rock Bud. I love you so very much!

To my readers, thank you for giving me that opportunity to share my struggles, my pain, and my healing. I hope you too have found light within the darkness.

With Love & Gratitude,

Vicki

About the Author

Vicki Savini is an international writer, speaker and life coach who empowers children and adults to be their absolute best by healing their deepest toxic belief. Her ground-breaking work has helped countless individuals to stop living in darkness and step out into the light. She has been featured in the Hay House Heal Your Life Blog, Tiny Buddha and SimpleReminders.com. Vicki lives in upstate New York with her amazing son and two lovable pups.

For more information on Vicki, go to

www.vickisavini.com